A PICTORIAL HISTORY
OF THE CONFEDERACY

A PICTORIAL HISTORY
of the
CONFEDERACY

BY

Lamont Buchanan

BONANZA BOOKS · NEW YORK

⊷{ CONTENTS }⊶

──❧{ FOREWORD }❧──

The compilation of this pictorial history of the years of the Confederacy is a story in itself. In those days of almost a century ago, photography was still a relatively new operation; not at all the commonplace, scientific, widely utilized reportorial device it is today. Then, the camera was used primarily to immortalize the stiffly posed likenesses of individuals and family groups, usually to be handed down only to an intimate and limited posterity.

The War Between the States produced the first famous "news" photographer—Mathew Brady—but he was a Northerner and thus his tremendously prolific camera gave, in the main, almost as one-sided a picture of history as a modern Signal Corps lensman. While the North had Brady with his staff and plentiful supplies of equipment and film, the comparatively few Southern photographers battled as vigorously against their own equipment shortages as did their fighting brothers in the field. Those who were able to continue in the business of taking photos did splendid work, though much of it was confined to picture portraits. As photographic supplies had to be smuggled in from the

North, excursions onto the fields of war were often frowned upon (except in the case of men like A. D. Lytle who managed to get photos of Union fortifications and forces for Confederate headquarters) when there was just so much film available and portraits of Postmaster General Reagan, Admiral Semmes, General Longstreet and others in demand.

Later, many of these photographers knew the final heartbreak of seeing much of their picture work destroyed by the occupation troops, along with other valuable records and archives of the times.

Despite such difficulties, the visual record of the war in the South is extraordinarily rich. In spite of the material restrictions of its economy, the Confederate States produced great quantities of printed matter in the form of posters, broadsides, circulars, almanacs, books, sheet music and calendars. Many were illustrated with drawings or paintings, lithographs and etchings, cartoons and caricatures, charts and maps, all providing a graphic comment on Confederate times, heroes, public figures, historic moments and places.

The back issues of Southern newspapers and periodicals of those times which were consulted are almost beyond counting; they have provided a splendid source of other background material from facts to fancies, from rumors to anecdotia.

The illustrative material in this book was culled from all these sources; literally tens of thousands of such pieces were examined in museums, libraries, historical societies, picture agencies, as well as other public and private collections.

A portion, like some of the Volck engravings, the Sheppard water colors, the Chapman oils, several of the Bradys are well-known and justly famous. Other material has never been reproduced since original publication during those bitter days of war.

This book is not a history book. It is not a "scholar's" lengthy reference work. Instead, it attempts to make a selective, illustrated presentation of the personalities—civilian as well as military—and their lives and problems; the bitter day-to-day struggles, the incredible sacrifice and the heroism that supported the brief life of the Confederacy.

The historic secession documents, the clarion calls of the newspapers for action, the vivid posters, the many scenes of high drama from homefront to battlefront, from the Montgomery inaugural and Sumter to the war's end—how well the tale can be traced visually!

In this pictorial volume, the brave people and fateful years of the Confederate States of America live again and the reader is eyewitness to exciting and poignant events without parallel in American history.

PICTURE CREDITS AND ACKNOWLEDGMENTS

The author wishes to extend his thanks to Dr. H. J. Eckenrode of Richmond, Virginia, who was kind enough to go over the manuscript and whose excellent suggestions have proved most helpful.

On matters of picture research the author is particularly in debt to Miss India W. Thomas of the Confederate Memorial Literary Society and the Confederate Museum in Richmond, a most gracious lady and an estimable scholar of the subject, whose advice and help in the collection of much pictorial matter was invaluable. In addition, thanks are due Miss Eleanor S. Brockenbrough, also of the Confederate Museum, whose generous assistance is much appreciated.

James A. Fleming, John Melville Jennings, the Reverend Clayton Torrence, and Miss Ellen B. Wooldridge of the Virginia Historical Society were very generous with their help in the collecting of other pictorial material.

For the illustrative matter made available by the Virginia State Library, the author wishes to extend his sincere appreciation to Randolph W. Church, as well as William J. Van Schreeven and Milton C. Russell.

The Valentine Museum in Richmond was the source of additional material, and the author wishes particularly to thank Mrs. Ralph Catterall and Mrs. Mary T. Pyle for their assistance.

The preponderance of pictures, illustrations and documents in this volume came from the following sources: The Bettmann Archive, Brown Brothers, The Confederate Museum, Culver Service, Harris & Ewing, Keystone View Company, New York Public Library, Underwood & Underwood, The Valentine Museum, Virginia Historical Society, and Virginia State Library.

Among the many persons and institutions throughout the South whose response and counsel have been appreciated, the author particularly wishes to thank the following:

Marie B. Owen, Alabama State Department of Archives and History, Montgomery, Alabama
Ruth Blair, Atlanta Historical Society, Atlanta, Georgia
Ellen M. FitzSimons, Charleston Library Society, Charleston, South Carolina
Henry E. Coleman, Jr., Cyrus Hall McCormick Library, Washington and Lee University, Lexington, Virginia
Dallas Historical Society, Dallas, Texas
B. E. Powell, Duke University Library, Durham, North Carolina
E. G. Roberts, The George Washington Flowers Memorial Collection, Duke University, Durham, North Carolina
Margaret Jemison, Emory University Library, Emory University, Georgia
Lilla M. Hawes, Georgia Historical Society, Savannah, Georgia
Mrs. J. E. Hays, Georgia State Department of Archives and History, Atlanta, Georgia
Lillian Patterson, The Georgia State Woman's College Library, Valdosta, Georgia
Garland F. Taylor, Howard-Tilton Memorial Library, Tulane University, New Orleans, Louisiana
Harry E. Pratt, Illinois State Historical Library, Springfield, Illinois
The Library of Congress, Washington, D. C.
Miriam Wetherbee, The Lincoln Library, Springfield, Illinois
Essae M. Culver, Louisiana State Library, Baton Rouge, Louisiana
S. Paul Revere, Louisiana State Museum, New Orleans, Louisiana
Ruth Campbell, Louisiana State University Library, Baton Rouge, Louisiana
Fred Shelley, Maryland Historical Society, Baltimore, Maryland
Nellie L. Glass, Montgomery Library Association, Montgomery, Alabama
The National Archives, Washington, D. C.
Mrs. John Trotwood Moore, Tennessee State Library and Archives, Nashville, Tennessee
Robert P. Quarles, Tennessee State Library and Archives, Nashville, Tennessee

Special thanks are also due Dr. Otto Bettmann of the Bettmann Archive, D. Jay Culver of Culver Service, and Miss Mary L. Manion of Brown Brothers, all of New York City, for their splendid cooperation and interest and for making available to the author the full facilities of their fine collections of historical matter.

For additional help with various research aspects, the author is indebted to A. I. Steinberg, as well as George T. Dove and Arthur J. Steffel.

A PICTORIAL HISTORY
OF THE CONFEDERACY

--⋙{ CHAPTER ONE }⋘--

Both North and South had combined to build the nation as it stood in the late 1850's; each region had contributed its own wealth of ingenuity, the strength of its sons, of its land and of its labor. Yet for several decades there were growing economic, cultural and psychological divisions between the two sections of the Union. The essential difference was in the very nature of the land and the economics imposed by natural advantages or limitations of environment. The South was primarily agricultural, while the North, in addition to resources of agriculture, had a growing industrial might fed by the steady stream of immigrants from across the seas. The North's greater commerce and communication with the rest of the world resulted in a less reverent attitude toward the traditional and established order. The complexities of heavily populated and urbanized communities required greater regulation and a bigger role for central government.

On the other hand stood the South's well-established pattern of agriculture, often referred to as a plantation society, a society that staunchly believed in states' rights, a somewhat laissez-faire economic system that resisted efforts toward greater Federal regulation. The South pointed with pride to its traditional culture and a graceful and prosperous way of life. It saw no need for change.

Jefferson Davis, who had given a large degree of self-government to his community of Mississippi plantation servants, and who found reason to believe that his well-fed staff of workers were happier and better cared for than the majority of the free workers of the North, was convinced that there was room in the new free states for the institution of slavery. On the other hand, Abraham Lincoln, though not the arch-abolitionist he was often pictured in the South, opposed the extension of slavery in the territories. These two tall, lean men spoke as moderates. They were courteous, gentle, admirable men—with ideas utterly at variance. Davis believed that any state had the right to secede from the Union; Lincoln held to the view that "a house divided against itself cannot stand." The debate, with slavery as its focal point, sounded in city streets, on courthouse steps in little towns, at crossroads; in Congress and in the newspaper columns of that day, in saloons as well as over kitchen tables.

It was a disturbing truth of the times that neither side fully appreciated the arguments—and the basic considerations from which these arguments stemmed—of the other. To be sure, there were many in the North who cried: "Let the Confederacy go in peace!" And there were those in the South who believed with equal fervor that the Union must be maintained, by arms if necessary. Still others, like President James Buchanan, hoped that some compromise could be found to stem the dangerous tide of dissension that rose after every major public utterance of each camp. Meetings, conferences and "peace conventions" were held, such as the one depicted above at Fort Scott in Kansas, portraying an incident during the border troubles preceding the War Between the States. Men of unquestioned sincerity and conviction lined up on both sides; the majority, at least outwardly, swore allegiance to a "peaceful solution," yet each group demanded that the peace must be preserved on terms agreeable to their own side, and many men of discernment recognized privately the drift toward violence as final arbiter of all disagreements.

Throughout both sections—North and South—trouble flared. There were fist fights between those who wished to exclude slavery from the territories and those who opposed such action. The Marais des Cygnes Massacre, indicated above, was but one of innumerable events to fan the flames of disunity. This incident of the Kansas Border War took place in May of 1858 when a settler from Georgia, with some companions, shot a number of Free State men near the Marais des Cygnes River. Whittier wrote a poem commemorating the event; it was token of the increasing friction between men of different opinion.

As the North argued bitterly against slavery, the people of the South, hearing themselves branded "medieval monsters opposed to freedom," solidified in defense of themselves and their institutions. Actually, there had been active anti-slavery groups in the South for many years. Contrary to Northern impression, not even one white in ten owned any slaves; many more Southern farms were operated by non-slaveholders than by slaveholders. Yet in the North the popular rallying issue was "Freedom for the slaves."

Seward's "irrepressible conflict" and Lincoln's "divided house" were both threat and condemnation to a South which felt the issue was its own freedom and that of a traditional way of life.

This cheering, hat-raising secession meeting took place in front of the venerable Mills House in Charleston, South Carolina, in late 1860. Whispers of secession had been heard for some time in South Carolina. Whispers became voices and now the voices were raised to a roar. Soon separation from the Union seemed a foregone conclusion. The only questions in the minds of many secessionists were: How? And when? The cautious—called timid by their friends, cowardly by their more extreme brethren—pointed out that should war come, the agricultural South, with its population of eight or nine million, must face an enemy with more than twenty million people, and further, an enemy rich in the tools and products of manufacture.

IMPORTANT FROM WASHINGTON!

Address of Senator TOOMS to the People of Georgia!

PROPOSITION FOR NEW GUARANTEES
REJÉCTED ::

THE SOUTH TREATED WITH DERISION & CONTEMPT

Senator Crittenden's Amendments UNANIMOUSLY VOTED DOWN!

SECESSION
The LAST and ONLY Resort!

Special Dispatch to the Constitutionalist.

WASHINTON, DEC. 23, 1860.

Senator Toombs telegraphs, this morning, the following, addressed to the people of Georgia:

Fellow-Citizens of Georgia:---I came here to secure your Constitutional rights, or to demonstrate to you that you can get no guarantees for these rights from your Northern confederates.

The whole subject was referred to a Committee of thirteen in the Senate yesterday. I was appointed on the committee and accepted the trust. I submitted propositions, which so far from receiving decided support from a single member of the Republican party on the committee, they were all treated with either derision or contempt. The vote was taken in committee on the amendments to the Constitution proposed by Hon. J. J. Crittenden, of Kentucky, and each and all of them were VOTED AGAINST UNANIMOUSLY by the Black Republican members of the committee.

In April of 1860 the regular Democratic Convention was held in Charleston. William Yancey of Alabama, sometimes called the "voice of secession," Rhett of South Carolina, and Toombs of Georgia, argued eloquently for what they felt was the political path the South must travel. When their plans failed of adoption by the narrowest of margins, the Cotton States withdrew their delegates from the convention; the dissenting Southern Democrats later nominated their own candidate in addition to the regular party choice, and a third party made an additional selection. Thus the voter of 1860 could choose between four slates. The resulting national vote was purely sectional and though the Republican ticket, headed by Lincoln, was victorious, his popular vote was about a million less than the combined total of his three opponents. Many Southerners, feeling themselves betrayed, unfurled their own flags (below) and shouted a challenge across the land.

Opposite, Bob Toombs, as fiery in print as he was in speech, thundered secession to the people of Georgia via wire from Washington, his words echoing the fears of the South. This was probably the last time Toombs's name was misspelled, as his voice was to be heard increasingly throughout the land.

Many persons above the Mason-Dixon line, from "professional" patriots to more sober thinkers, viewed the secession movement with some satisfaction, believing that a clear-cut issue giving an excuse for force would thereby provide its own solution. They believed the secessionists were putting themselves inescapably out on a limb; cartoonists and caricaturists of the times delighted in drawing elaborate pictures of what they visualized as the plight of the South if it were to cut itself off from the Union. But regardless of consequences, most South Carolinians felt that secession was the way now dictated by honor and circumstances. Meanwhile, in Charleston Harbor, Federal soldiers on Sullivan's Island (below) heard whispered rumors that they might be attacked by state militia.

There were bleak November skies overhead when word of Abraham Lincoln's election in 1860 reached Richmond and spread through the Southern states. The news, considered "shocking" by many, caused the state legislature of South Carolina to ask delegates to act upon the issue of secession. In December the convention met, and by unanimous vote South Carolina withdrew from the Union.

With the threatened secession of South Carolina now a fact, urgent
messages asking for reinforcements came to Washington from Major
Robert Anderson, in command of U. S. installations in Charleston Harbor. President James Buchanan, appalled at the thought of war between
North and South, was indecisive. His own Attorney General had
handed down an opinion that the President had the right to protect
property of the United States wherever that might be, by the dispatch
of armed forces if necessary. Still, Buchanan hoped for compromise;
he feared that Federal reinforcements to such centers of secession as
Charleston would bring matters to a boil. Meantime, Major Anderson
ordered his small force to Fort Sumter on December 26th, and in the
deepening twilight soldiers and provisions were shifted silently across

the 1,000 yards of dark water to the bastion in the middle of the harbor. Though its barracks were unfinished, its three gun tiers without their full complement of cannon, Anderson felt Sumter was more defensible than any of the other Federal strongholds, Castle Pinckney, and Forts Johnson and Moultrie.

Major Anderson's quarters on Sumter, sketched by one of his officers. Anderson, who had already served with valor as an Indian fighter, was a Kentuckian by birth, married to a Southern girl, and considered to be a "pro-slavery man." At the same time he brooded about the secession issue, privately told companions-in-arms that he opposed the "Southern extremists" and was against an individual state or group of states seceding from the Union. Major Anderson felt his first duty was to follow orders—hold the Federal forts against an aggression. If Pinckney, Johnson and Moultrie could not be effectively defended, then he would hold the island fort of Sumter as long as possible. The defenses on Sumter were incomplete, but the island offered much better opportunity for resistance should an attack occur.

ABBEVILLE
BANNER
EXTRA.

Passed unanimously at 1.15 o'clock, P. M. December 20th, 1860.

AN ORDINANCE

To dissolve the Union between the State of South Carolina and other States united with her under the compact entitled " The Constitution of the United States of America."

We, the People of the State of South Carolina, in Convention assembled, do declare and ordain, and it is hereby declared and ordained,

That the Ordinance adopted by us in Convention, on the twenty-third day of May, in the year of our Lord one thousand seven hundred and eighty-eight, whereby the Constitution of the United States of America was ratified, and also, all Acts and parts of Acts of the General Assembly of this State, ratifying amendments of the said Constitution, are hereby repealed; and that the union now subsisting between South Carolina and other States, under the name of " The United States of America," is hereby dissolved.

THE
UNION
IS
DISSOLVED!

Huge newspaper headlines, such as these from the Abbeville, South Carolina *Banner*, announcing that state's dissolution of the "union subsisting between South Carolina and other States under the name of The United States of America," preceded by but a few weeks similar action from other states. Commencing early in 1861, Mississippi, Florida, Alabama, Georgia, Louisiana and Texas followed South Carolina's example. This copy of the original Ordinance of Secession of the "Republic of Georgia" records for history the names of the signers plus six delegates who "most solemnly Protest against the action of the majority . . . yet as good citizens we yield to the will of a majority." On February fourth six of the states (Texas' delegates had been unable to reach the convention in time) met in Montgomery, Alabama, formed the Confederate States of America, drafted a tentative Constitution and chose a provisional President.

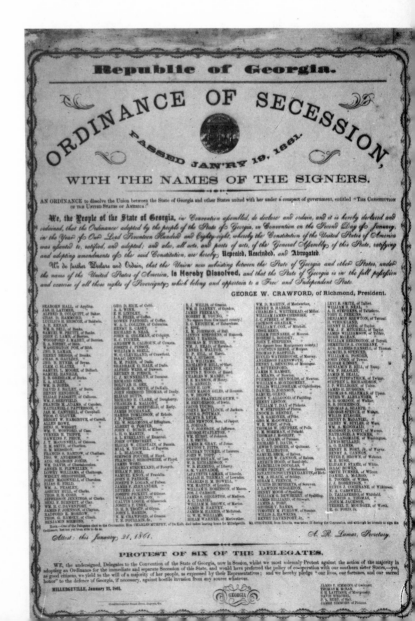

Huge newspaper headlines, such as these from the Abbeville, South Carolina *Banner*, announcing that state's dissolution of the "union subsisting between South Carolina and other States under the name of The United States of America," preceded by but a few weeks similar action from other states. Commencing early in 1861, Mississippi, Florida, Alabama, Georgia, Louisiana and Texas followed South Carolina's example. This copy of the original Ordinance of Secession of the "Republic of Georgia" records for history the names of the signers plus six delegates who "most solemnly Protest against the action of the majority . . . yet as good citizens we yield to the will of a majority." On February fourth six of the states (Texas' delegates had been unable to reach the convention in time) met in Montgomery, Alabama, formed the Confederate States of America, drafted a tentative Constitution and chose a provisional President.

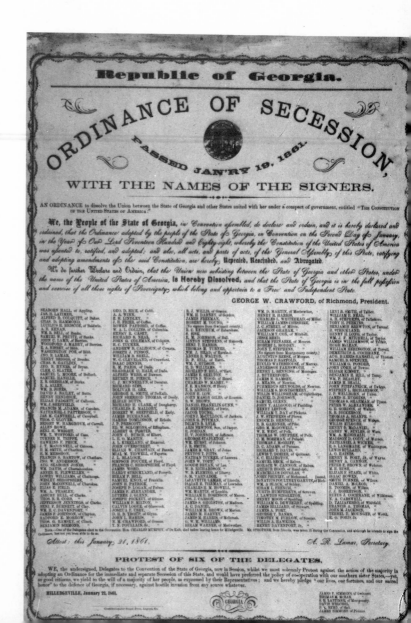

To head the seven states of the Lower South, the delegates at Montgomery chose Jefferson Davis, who had attended West Point and served the United States well in the Mexican War. Occupying the post of Secretary of War from 1853 to 1857 in the cabinet of President Pierce, Davis also had considerable experience in government as both congressman and senator from Mississippi. For some time he had been associated in many minds with the cotton interests and, fairly, as their spokesman. But up until the word came from Montgomery, Jefferson Davis had shown little ambition for a government position with the seceded states. Davis supported the "status quo"; as a Southern gentleman he felt it almost a requirement of honor that a majority opinion of that region would be his opinion. However, when word came from Alabama, his wife, who was at his side, spoke of the look of sadness that crossed his face as he opened the communique which revealed that he was to serve as head of the government instead of as the leader of the Mississippi Army. Throughout his career Davis fancied himself as a military expert of no inconsiderable talent, and during his years of office would sometimes escape to the field of battle as a release from governing a young nation whose problems multiplied with the passing months.

Much as he would have liked an army command, Jefferson Davis was destined for an even more ambitious role, and on February 9th he was elected first President of the Confederate States. On the same day Alexander Stephens, the frail little Georgian who was torn between belief in the Union and in states' rights, was elected Vice-President. Two days before the inaugural at Montgomery on the 18th, the new President stood tall and erect before cheering throngs as Yancey introduced him. . . . "The man and the hour have met."

Davis' cabinet was to undergo many changes during its comparatively brief lifetime, but at first it was geographically if not characteristically representative of the South it pledged to serve. Stephen Mallory of Florida was appointed Secretary of the Navy; Christopher Memminger of South Carolina became Secretary of the Treasury; John Reagan of Texas, Postmaster General; Leroy Pope Walker of Alabama, Secretary of War; Robert Toombs of Georgia, Secretary of State, and Judah Benjamin of Louisiana, Attorney General.

THE RIGHT MAN, IN THE RIGHT PLACE.

JEFF. DAVIS.

OUR FIRST PRESIDENT.

There were vexing problems to be faced by Davis, "Our First President," after the hand-portraits, posters and buttons of inaugural excitement were put aside. As the states had seceded, each had seized United States forts and military posts within its borders. Thus they held sixteen army posts, mostly in Texas, while only four of any importance within Southern borders remained in Yankee hands—Sumter, Pickens, and Dry Tortugas and Key West in Florida. In order to handle the disputes rising from their seizures and from the Southern states' insistence on seizing the posts within their territories, agents were dispatched to Washington to confer with President Buchanan. However, most of them arrived so late that it then seemed advisable to wait until the new President was inaugurated.

On March 4th, two weeks after Jefferson Davis, the man of Mississippi, met his destiny in Montgomery, another man took the oath of office in Washington. As Abraham Lincoln was inaugurated, the *Richmond Enquirer* came out with an edition adorned with heavy black mourning borders. Even though still nominally aligned with the Union, Richmond feared that Lincoln meant to save the United States by abolitionists' methods. Virginia's sympathies were unmistakable. In his inaugural Lincoln said: "I have no intention of interfering with slavery where it now exists. . . ." But the South did not believe.

Even before either of the new Presidents was inaugurated, Virginia was anticipating a perilous future. Impatient at the delay in joining their seceding brethren, some Virginia patriots started to organize their own companies. Young men were called to volunteer, while property owners were expected to offer money or whatever goods were available and most needed. All this was done unofficially, somewhat surreptitiously, in fact. For even while the Confederate States of America was being formed in Montgomery, Virginia was issuing an invitation for all states to take part in a peace conference. Richmond seethed with rumors and impatience. Governor Letcher had proclaimed that the state would resist the passage over her borders of any troops sent to coerce a secessionist state. But he also called for days of prayer "that a calamity shall not befall us." Some prayed; some muttered that they would never allow "the Africanization of our Virginia."

VOLUNTEERS WANTED!

I wish to enroll immediately 50 young Unmarried men in Company "A," who will be READY and WILLING to defend Virginia from the Abolitionists of the North, when called for by our Governor.

W. H. WERTH,
Commandant Company "A," 101st Regiment.

TO THE CITIZENS OF PITTSYLVANIA COUNTY:

PITTSYLVANIA COURT HOUSE, January, 1861.

FELLOW CITIZENS:

From all indications we are upon the eve of a civil war, which in less than ninety days, may bring down upon the soil of Virginia an army of Abolitionists under orders from Abraham Lincoln, the then President of the Northern United States, and deluge our land in blood; to desolate our homes, and leave the State of our birth a wilderness and ruin. These things may not overtake us, but from all the sources of information presented to our view, the *strong probabilities* are that such will be our fate as soon as Lincoln is inaugurated, unless we place ourselves in a complete state of military defence. With this awful reality staring us in the face; with the full *knowledge* that the Abolitionists of our neighbor State, Pennsylvania, are forming Volunteer Companies for the express purpose of "*operating against the South;*" with the knowledge that the *four hundred thousand* Abolition "Wide Awakes," who aided and gloried in Lincoln's election, are forming themselves into Military organizations for the sole purpose of "*compelling the submission of the South at the point of the bayonet;*" with the knowledge that General Winfield Scott, the senior officer in the United States Army, is *advising* and using all his influence to induce the President to blockade the sea ports of the South, and to station large bodies of troops in the heart of *all the Southern States,* for the purpose of robbing us of all the rights which are dear to us as freemen; with the *knowledge* that the Abolition Abe Lincoln, has declared through his representatives, that as soon as he is inaugurated, he will use all the power of the Army and Navy to subdue the Southern States who dare to assert their rights as freemen; with the *knowledge* that they of the Northern States are putting themselves upon a "*war footing,*" for this "*invasion of the South;*" with the *knowledge* that Congress has totally failed to invent any plan by which the hostility between the North and South can be allayed, and have discharged both of their Peace Committees in despair;—*all* of these things send their warnings to us and conjure us to prepare to DEFEND OUR HOMES, OUR LIVES, OUR WIVES AND CHILDREN, OUR LIBERTY, AND OUR PROPERTY. *Inaction, apathy,* or a further disposition to "*wait,*" is *treason* to Virginia, perfidy to our friends; and *cruel brutality* to our wives and children. The young men who are willing to enter the "Tented Field," in defence of Virginia, are generally poor and unable to purchase a complete outfit for the field; they are ready to risk their lives for our homes and our families, provided they be supplied with the necessary outfit for *active service;* and it is the duty of the older citizens, the property-holders, those who have their all at stake, to come to the aid of the Volunteers, and by their liberal contributions in money, furnish such things as the Volunteers will require. We, therefore, feeling the necessity of *instant preparation,* propose a mass meeting of our fellow citizens at January Court at this place, for the purpose of raising an amount sufficient to pay for the uniforms, &c., of all such young men as may attach themselves to Light Infantry Company "A," 101st Regiment, commanded by Capt. W. H. WERTH, and who may be unable to pay for the same; also an amount sufficient to purchase knapsacks, blankets, &c., &c., for the same Company, until it shall fill up its ranks to 100 strong. We call upon the heads of families, the *property-owners* of the county, those who will be unable to do service, to come up to the aid of the Volunteers, and contribute liberally to their wants, either at the meeting at January Court, or when called upon by one of the Committee to collect.

Respectfully, &c.,

CITIZENS OF PITTSYLVANIA.

While Virginians were preparing themselves and their state as best they could in a twilight period between Union and secession and a possible invasion of their soil by "an army of Abolitionists under orders from Abraham Lincoln," events were rapidly on the march in the deeper South. South Carolinians were concerned with the presence of the Union troops on their harbor doorstep. A newly appointed Brigadier General of the Confederate States Army soon appeared in Charleston to prepare for the forceful eviction of the Union troops and to protect the harbor from Federal reinforcements. The new arrival, originally from New Orleans and of French extraction, was Pierre Gustave Toutant Beauregard. To certain fluttering female hearts of the community, he was the personification of a gallant and dashing officer. But Anderson, on Sumter, knew other things about Beauregard which, if they did not cause heart flutterings, certainly did cause misgivings. For Beauregard, as a cadet at West Point, had studied under the tutelage of Anderson himself, and was remembered as a brilliant student of artillery.

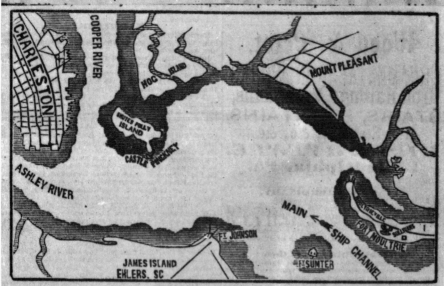

FORT SUMTER.

Lies about one mile from the shore, directly on the main ship channel, which passes between the Fort, and Sullivan's Island, on which is located Fort Moultrie, about one mile distant. From the battery of Charleston city, Fort Sumter lies about five miles distant, standing out in the open bay, one mile from the land on either side. Fort Moultrie is, in military phrase, commanded by Fort Sumter. The latter is a casemated fortification, similar to that now in construction in the Patapsco river, on Sollers' Flats, whilst Fort Moultrie is an open work like Fort McHenry, but of smaller size.

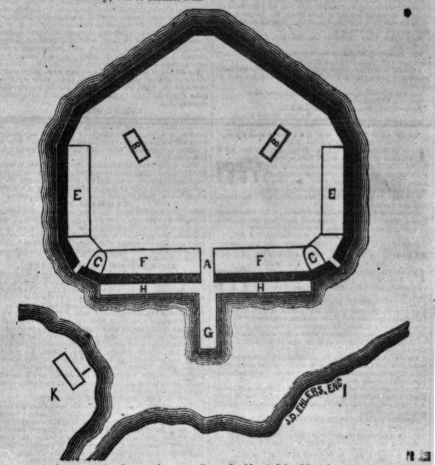

A—Arched gateway in the southwest wall.
B—Furnaces for heating shot.
C—Powder magazines.
D—Sally ports.
E—Barracks for the soldiers.
F—Officers' quarters.
G—Wharf; depth of water on east side 16 to 18 feet
H—Principal landing; extending along the entire southwest wall.

I—Morris Island beach.
K—Old Barracks on James Island (Fort Johnson.)

We would mention that the position of Morris and James Islands, owing to the small size of the engraving, is not intended to be considered as more than indicating their proximity to Fort Sumter.

Sumter seemed the key to Southern determination for states' rights. And Beauregard was the wielder of the key. The young general set out immediately to fortify the harbor against threat of reinforcements from the sea. Lincoln and his new government watched the situation carefully but did nothing. Davis likewise marked time. But Carolinians wanted action and threatened to precipitate matters if their Montgomery government did not. Jefferson Davis complained to intimates that the issue was being "needlessly forced" but on April 11th, after three days of fruitless negotiations, the surrender of Sumter was demanded. Earlier, wives and children of men belonging to the Fort Moultrie garrison were ordered from Charleston and waved tearful farewells as their craft steamed slowly past the fort on the way out of the harbor for the North.

Surrounded by batteries on Morris Island, James Island and Fort Johnson, plus more cannon directed at Sumter from Fort Moultrie on Sullivan's Island, Anderson realized defense was hopeless. Yet when the surrender of Sumter was officially demanded, the Major refused and passed the word to his men that the time for fighting was nearly upon them.

31

All through the night of April 11th both sides waited. Citizens of Charleston and from the surrounding countryside gathered on the shores in great excitement to watch the expected spectacle. But when midnight came and went with no noise but the murmurs of watching people, the crowd dispersed. Finally at 4:30 A.M., a warning gun was fired from nearby Fort Johnson (left). Soon after, the mortar battery on Morris Island opened up on Sumter. All during the day of the 12th, and through the next night, the remarkably accurate bombardment by the Confederates continued. On the 13th, fires were started in the fort (above) as batteries from Fort Moultrie, at left, and Cummings Point, right, continued to lob their explosives onto the island. At seven in the evening Major Anderson surrendered. While firing a last salute to the U. S. flag, one of Sumter's cannon burst, killing a soldier and wounding five more. These were the only casualties of the bombardment, and the first of the much greater conflict that was to spread from Charleston Harbor as though with the winds that blew smoke and flame from Sumter across the sky.

An Ordinance

To repeal the ratification of the Constitution of the United States of America by the State of Virginia, and to resume all the rights and powers granted under said Constitution.

The people of Virginia, in their ratification of the Constitution of the United States of America, adopted by them in Convention on the twenty fifth day of June in the year of our Lord one thousand seven hundred and eighty eight having, declared that the powers granted under the said Constitution, were derived from the people of the United States and might be resumed whensoever the same should be perverted to their injury and oppression and the Federal Government having perverted said powers not only to the injury of the people of Virginia, but to the oppression of the Southern Slaveholding States.

Now, therefore, we, the people of Virginia, do declare and ordain. That the ordinance adopted by the people of this State in Convention on the twenty fifth day of June in the year of our Lord one thousand seven hundred and eighty eight whereby the Constitution of the United States of America was ratified, and all acts of the General Assembly of this State ratifying or adopting amendments to said Constitution, are hereby **repealed and abrogated,** that the union between the State of Virginia and other States under the Constitution aforesaid is hereby dissolved, and that the State of Virginia is in the full possession and exercise of all the rights of sovereignty which belong and appertain to a **free and independent State.**

And they do further declare, That said Constitution of the United States of America is no longer binding on any of the citizens of this State.

This ordinance shall take effect and be an act of this day when ratified by a majority of the votes of the people of this State, cast at a poll to be taken thereon on the fourth Thursday in May next in pursuance of a Schedule hereafter to be enacted.

Done in Convention in the City of Richmond on the seventeenth day of April, in the year of our Lord one thousand eight hundred and sixty one and in the eighty fifth year of the **Commonwealth of Virginia.**

Attest

Jno. L. Eubank

Secretary of the Convention.

After the fall of Fort Sumter, Abraham Lincoln called for 75,000 troops to be raised for the purpose of "repossessing the forts, places and property which have been seized from the Union." This requisition met with immediate opposition in the Border States of the South. Two days after Lincoln's request, on April 17th the Virginia State Convention adopted its Ordinance of Secession (though it was not to be ratified by the voters for more than a month), and promptly state forces moved on the Arsenal at Harper's Ferry (above). Though the Yankees had fired it when word of the impending seizure reached them, some valuable machinery and small arms were captured. To Virginians, to Southerners, Harper's Ferry had a special significance beyond any mere military value. For it was here, in 1859, that John Brown, with some followers, had invaded Virginia and tried to start a general slave insurrection. In much of the North he became a martyr, yet Brown was reportedly less interested in the "cause" for which he had been enlisted than in any opportunity for violence. And it probably bothered him considerably less than his monied backers that not one slave had willingly joined the self-appointed liberators.

Harper's Ferry seemed in a perpetual state of alarm and violence. Its position astride the vital B&O railroad to the West made it the key if not the prize of several campaigns and innumerable sorties. To a South in greater supply of willingness than of the material sinews of war, it

was cause for cheer when Thomas Jonathan Jackson, later the fabulous "Stonewall," swept down on the railroad near Harper's Ferry and made away with a number of locomotives and considerable rolling stock. Shown above is a historic landmark, the U. S. armory which John Brown and his men captured briefly in mid-October of 1859, still a notorious site at Harper's Ferry.

As soon as Virginia's secession became official, Union troops crossed into the northwestern part of the state to protect strategic railroad lines against attack, and, coincidentally, thereby helped to bring into existence the new state of West Virginia on the side of the North. At the same time soldiers pressed down from Washington to occupy Arlington Heights and Alexandria, both precious to the Lees. And Major General Benjamin Butler, stationed at Fortress Monroe (above foreground) at the mouth of the James River, started a carefully planned advance up the slender peninsula toward Richmond.

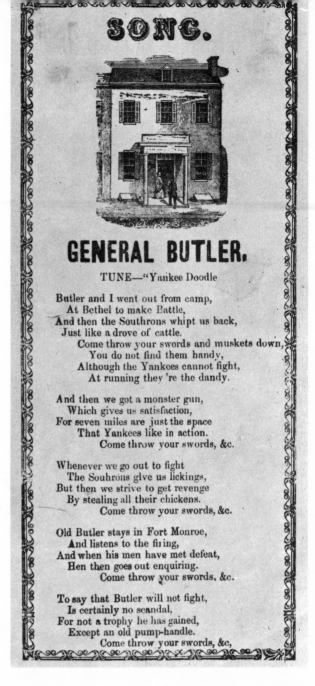

SONG.

GENERAL BUTLER.

TUNE—"Yankee Doodle

Butler and I went out from camp,
    At Bethel to make Battle,
And then the Southrons whipt us back,
    Just like a drove of cattle.
        Come throw your swords and muskets down,
            You do not find them handy,
        Although the Yankees cannot fight,
            At running they're the dandy.

And then we got a monster gun,
    Which gives us satisfaction,
For seven miles are just the space
    That Yankees like in action.
        Come throw your swords, &c.

Whenever we go out to fight
    The Souhrons glve us lickings,
But then we strive to get revenge
    By stealing all their chickens.
        Come throw your swords, &c.

Old Butler stays in Fort Monroe,
    And listens to the firing,
And when his men have met defeat,
    Hen then goes out enquiring.
        Come throw your swords, &c.

To say that Butler will not fight,
    Is certainly no scandal,
For not a trophy he has gained,
    Except an old pump-handle.
        Come throw your swords, &c,

Butler's men had considerable difficulty working up toward Richmond. Though enemy forces had been steadily increasing in the Fortress Monroe area, opposed by John B. Magruder, at this early stage of the war the fighting qualities of Northern troops were suspect. It was thought in some quarters that the Union used "mercenaries" or went to great lengths to impress "volunteers" into service. Some of the early brushes between soldiers of both sides seemed to bear out the assumption that the Yankees could not match Southerners in fighting ability. A sarcastic poem set to music and dedicated to General Butler was widely read by amused readers who told one another that the verse "had more than a smidgin of truth."

CHAPTER TWO

F EW CASUAL ACQUAINTANCES, knowing the gentle yet unbending
character of Robert E. Lee in performance of his duties, could
guess the intense struggle that this valiant hero of the War Between the States had waged with himself at the outset of those hostilities.
Lee, a professional soldier of the highest attainments, had been suggested
as commander of the United States forces. In a tumult of feeling he
had refused command of the Federal Army and resigned his commission
for "I cannot raise my hand against my birthplace. . . ." so setting himself free to serve his native Virginia. Meanwhile, war news filled columns
in the papers as the various states, like men, struggled with their con-
sciences to determine the right and honorable course each should follow.

In some areas, particularly key Border States like Tennessee, Kentucky and Missouri (shown), the division of opinion threatened counties, towns and even families. The instance of Senator George Crittenden of Kentucky was not unusual. Of three sons, all young men of high character, two served the Union, the other the Confederacy. In Missouri soon after Fort Sumter, a brush between state militia and Federal troops at Lindell's Grove inflamed the entire area. People who had said in moderation: "Wait and see," now militantly took sides.

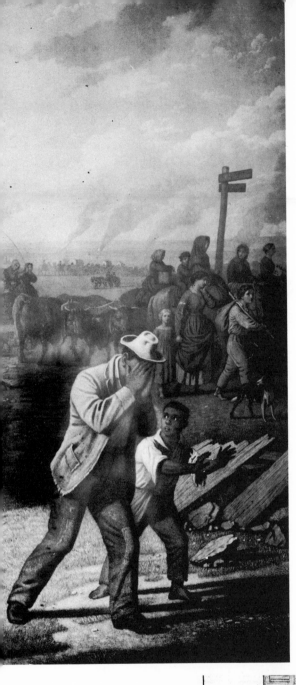

Captain Nathaniel Lyon of the Union Army touched off the trouble at Camp Jackson, Lindell's Grove, just outside St. Louis. Lyon feared that Missouri militia, known to be of secessionist sympathies, were awaiting a chance to seize the Federal arsenal and bring St. Louis itself under control. Later, Lyon and his United States volunteers marched the state militiamen, now as prisoners, into the city where crowds viewed the spectacle with mixed emotions. Soon firing started between the U. S. troops and spectators. Groups of men and boys armed with makeshift weapons and not a few muzzleloaders, crying "Hoorah for Missouri!", pelted the Federals with rocks and shot. It was a night of rioting in St. Louis. The terror continued until the "moderate" Union General Harney returned, took over from fiery Captain Lyon, assured the populace they were in no danger and urged everyone "to go home."

"When the hour of danger comes, we may lay aside the robes of legislature, buckle on the armor of the soldier. . . ." So spoke Howell Cobb as he addressed the Confederate Senate in open session (above) in Montgomery, Alabama, arguing for the removal of the capital to Richmond where it would be close at hand to the fighting men in the forward posts. Cobb, an influential Georgia planter, felt with many others that the move to Virginia's chief city was most important. In a South that revered military prowess and the honor and romance thereupon attendant, the psychological value of placing the seat of government and its President near to the battlefields was not to be underestimated. Accordingly, late in May of 1861, Richmond was voted the new capital of the Confederacy though some thought it was a bad choice, being too far from the Lower South.

Robert Toombs, heading the Confederate State Department, was by experience a financial expert, by temperament a fiery extremist, and soon, by taste, a critic of Jefferson Davis. Toombs had already called Davis "an incompetent" and thundered advice and censure in many directions. Davis' supporters claimed that Toombs would readily disagree with anyone . . . even with himself!

Both North and South considered Maryland a vitally important territory. Northern military officials well realized that control of Maryland meant control of the whole Chesapeake area, while loss of that state would further imperil the defense of Washington itself. After an anti-Union mob had attacked troops of the Sixth Massachusetts in Baltimore, Lincoln ordered such active and violent secessionists "constrained at any cost." Despite suppressive measures, many Marylanders escaped with "goods, guns, and ammunition" to row across the Potomac, bent on joining the Confederate armies, as in the Adalbert Volck engraving, at right. In Southern Maryland, it was not at all uncommon for Federal troops to swoop down on a private home known to house secessionist sympathizers in search for arms which sometimes were found secreted in the rooms of lovely maidens, whose innocent smiles would turn to frowns as a sword or gun was uncovered by the "meddlesome Yankees."

TO ARMS!
To Arms! To Arms!
Defend your Homes and Firesides.

THREE HUNDRED ABLE-BODIED YOUNG MEN are wanted to meet in LEXINGTON, on SATURDAY, APRIL 20th, 1861, to form three Companies of VOLUNTEERS for the defence of Virginia against the invasion threatened by her Northern foes. Your State is in danger. Rally to her Standard.

Lexington, April 17, 1861.

48

Signs of the times appeared and were noted by a citizenry still somewhat bewildered by the swift movement of events and the equally swift accrual of responsibilities. In the spring of 1861, the fancy of young and old alike in Virginia not-so-lightly turned to thoughts of defense as noted in the poster opposite, while below, recruiting for the Confederate Army goes forward with drum and fife.

"When the last line of bayonets is leveled, I will be with you," President Jefferson Davis once said to some troops. It was a gala occasion when Davis, a soldier at heart himself, and the government he headed arrived in Richmond. Gaily clad spectators lined the way to the Spotswood Hotel—to be used briefly as the executive mansion—as the sound of tolling church bells mingled with the thunder of cannon. Large numbers in the throng had not seen the President previously, and many were the remarks heard about the splendid appearance of the chief executive.

Mrs. Davis also excited much favorable comment. Some seventeen years younger than her husband, Varina Davis was a striking young woman, dark-haired and pleasantly featured, a good subject for photography or painting, above. On first meeting Jefferson Davis, she had written her mother, who was of Virginia lineage, that he was "a splendid gentleman, well-mannered even though he is a Democrat." Those graces were on exhibition, according to one story, as the two were driven toward the Spotswood when a large bouquet of flowers, tossed at the carriage for Mrs. Davis, fell short. President Davis immediately ordered a halt while he got out, retrieved the flowers himself and presented them to his wife. There was a ripple of pleased approval from the watching crowd and much hand-clapping as the procession again got under way.

Late in April of 1861, Lincoln declared a blockade of all Southern ports. The Union could continue to supplement its domestic output with imports from across oceans kept open for Northern shipping, even as Confederate sea commerce, insufficient anyway, was to be further hampered. The blockade served to unite the people and cement feelings of opposition in the South. Songwriters expressed popular sentiment, treated the United States as a foreign country and wrote pieces like the one (opposite) "Respectfully dedicated to the Army & Navy of the Confederate States of America."

Later on, an ordnance sergeant of the Confederate Army was to sketch this water color of one phase of the Union blockade, at Corpus Christi in Texas. Some Southern officials kept hoping that Mexico, just across the blue waters of the Gulf, might become an ally to the Confederate cause, but the presence of Federal ships-at-war was a deterrent. Texas, with its resources in manpower and food sometimes funneled toward the eastern states by way of New Orleans and sea avenues therefrom, was well worth the close attention of Union steamers and frigates, often seen patroling offshore from Galveston to Corpus Christi.

Meantime, on the home front, a Southern merchant, who could always blame the blockade for some of the things he didn't have, advertised with a sense of humor that business would go on despite secession. Far less humorous were posted warnings of the deadly penalty for treason.

52

TREASON IN VIRGINIA.

The Code of Virginia defines treason to be

"In levying war against the State, adhering to its enemies, or giving them aid and comfort."

Such treason, if proved by two witnesses, is punishable by death.

MAY 15, 1861.

FAREWELL To The STAR SPANGLED BANNER

ARRANGED FOR PIANO FORTE & GUITAR

RESPECTFULLY DEDICATED TO THE ARMY & NAVY OF THE C.S.A

RICHMOND PUBLISHED BY
J.W. DAVIES & SONS
199 MAIN ST
X Crehan Lith

SECESSION OF THE SOUTH
BUT NO DISSOLUTION OF BUSINESS.

ESTABLISHED IN 1837.

A. BAILEY

Has been battling ever since 1837 with the times, (occasionally wounding his BEST FRIENDS with a side glance,) and is still using his best efforts to serve them.

You who have stood by him in six troubles and in the seventh have not forsaken him—you who have ever extended to him an open purse with the most confiding courtesy, will please accept of an open hand and most grateful heart for the many favors bestowed by a troup of customers which no merchant ever had to excel and few to equal.

AT OLD ROUGH CREEK

You will find all the NECESSARIES and most of the luxuries at the lowest price for CASH or to prompt buyers.

Call at your earliest convenience and DEMAND the services of your much obliged friend and faithful and most obedient servant,

April 10th, 1861.   A. BAILEY.

The Southern states displayed remarkable ingenuity and energy. If a needed article could not be produced, a substitute was found. Despite a notorious shortage of machine tools, new mills were constructed and great amounts of war goods were turned out. This adaptability of an economy and a people became ever more important as the blockade grew tighter, almost completely cutting off any importation of steel and iron, munitions and other supplies from the Continent and England. Though the capital of Richmond still had its gay life and splendid parades as new troops passed through, the women here, as elsewhere in the South, turned to tasks which seemed foreign to some of them. Offices and living quarters were turned into sewing rooms to make what there was go further and last longer. Yet drygoods and fancy prints from overseas still made their way on occasion into the South and people took cheer from the arrival of such shipments, saying that after all, "The Yankees can't stop us from getting what we need."

All you needed to join the cavalry was a horse, went the saying. Others joked that if a man had the makings of a uniform and a gun, he was a soldier, and if he had a sword, a sash and a fine plumed hat, he could be an officer. Oversimplified, certainly, were these parodies on the process of military selection, yet the jokes had strong roots in the very real and basic restrictions of the South. Who, for instance, had heard of any man turning up with his own animal and being rejected by the horse troop? The outfitting of volunteers in any sort of style was often most difficult. In some counties the women made the uniforms; in others the government paid the volunteers a uniform allowance, and the men were supposed to clothe themselves as best they could.

During the earliest period of the war, the conflict was both a stimulation and an emotional release to many in the South, compounded of such excitements as flagwaving, gay uniforms and the dashing men who wore them, sentimental songs, social gatherings and parades. After Manassas, a part of whose Confederate fortifications are shown opposite, the large number of casualties sharply brought home to people everywhere the grim truths of war. Manassas was largely an end-result of the first "On to Richmond" drive of Union troops under McDowell. Often the geography of railroads predetermined where battles would take place, and the Orange & Alexandria RR lines, shown below at Union Mills Station near Bull Run, provided an avenue for movement and invasion.

57

First Manassas (or Bull Run) has often been called a battle of errors on both sides with victory going to the army that committed the fewest mistakes. Errors were to be expected. Both armies were newly organized, officered mainly by those who knew more about the theoretics of warfare than the actual practice. Joseph E. Johnston brought soldiers to Manassas by train, one of the first instances in which troops were conveyed to a battle by railway. In the middle of that warm July afternoon of 1861, Beauregard made a final effort, and the Union troops began to give way. Finally what started as an orderly withdrawal to Centreville became a rout as the retreating soldiers clogged the escape roads and mingled with "sightseers" who, reportedly, had come from the environs of Washington to witness the Confederate Army smashed with one great blow. Some Union forces fought bravely, gave ground grudgingly (below), while other depictions were less complimentary, telling of streams of U. S. troops fleeing as fast as they could down the congested Centreville turnpike, hotly pursued by the foe.

At first no one knew for sure why the Confederate troops did not follow their advantage even before the dust had settled along the lanes and paths of retreat. On the battlefield there was considerable confusion. Some units crossed Bull Run and made as if to pursue McDowell, but these forces were not augmented and were soon recalled. President Davis himself came to the front and considered the situation, finally concluding that "our men are not in such condition of supply and vigor as to turn immediately to pursuit and attack." In this decision the military seemed to concur, and some papers editorialized after-the-fact that "perhaps a great opportunity for Southern arms was not fully exploited." One thing made clear by Manassas was that the conflict would not soon be over.

In Washington Lincoln, grieving, wrote for his own eyes only the following affirmation and summing-up:

"The will of God prevails. In great contests each party claims to act in accordance with the will of God. Both may be, and one must be, wrong. God cannot be for and against the same thing at the same time. In the present civil war it is quite possible that God's purpose is something different from the purpose of either party; and yet the human instrumentalities, working just as they do, are the best adaptations to effect His purpose. I am almost ready to say that this is probably true; that God wills this contest and wills that it shall not end yet. By His mere great power on the minds of the now contestants, He could have either saved or destroyed the Union without a human contest. Yet the contest began. And, having begun, He could give the final victory to either side any day. Yet the contest proceeds."

In the ranks and among the officers there had been heavy losses at Bull Run, the most grievous of which was that of General Bee whose claim to fame, aside from his bravery, comes from his rallying cry to his men during the battle: "There stands Jackson like a stone wall. . . ." And from then on, it was as though Jackson (above) had shed his rightful name of Thomas Jonathan to become forever "Stonewall."

The Confederates did not spend much time brooding over what might have been at Manassas. Had they not won the first big battle of the war? Had not the Yankees been driven back and sent helter-skelter toward Washington? There was time, after Bull Run, for artistically inclined Southern soldiers to make sketches, like this one in pencil of a Confederate camp at Neils Dam. And not long after Manassas, General Magruder, who had faced Butler with success at Big Bethel earlier, stormed into the village of Hampton, Virginia, at the head of six hundred men, setting fire to buildings, and destroying several hundred of the wood-frame structures, below.

OLD ABE LINCOLN!

My name it is Abe Lincoln,
　I lead a wretched life,
I come from Springfield, Illinois,
　Me and my dear wife.
We brought with us our dear son Bob,
　To let the people know,
That the country I would plunder and rob,
　Where ever I would go.

When we arrived at New York,
　The people there were glad,
They paid me so much attention,
　I thought they 'ed drive me mad.
There was dinners, balls and parties,
　And every thing you know,
So then to good old Harrisburgh,
　I did resolve to go.

When I got to that city,
　I was so much scared,
That I'de never get through Baltimore,
　I was very much afraid.
But with my Scotch cap and military cloak,
　I thought I was all right,
And I slipped through that city,
　'Bout twelve o'clock at night.

So I fooled the Plug Uglies,
　As nice as ever could be,
For 'till one o'clock the next day,
　They were gaping and looking for me.
But I was snug in Washington,
　With Seward by my side,
And left my wife and my son Bob,
　On that fated train to ride.

But now here all safe with me,
　With two hundred thousand men,
That run away from Bull Run,
　And I am afraid they'll do it again.
For old General Scott has got the gout,
　And cant go in the field,
And the Generals now in the army,
　Aint fit a tin sword to wield.

BEAUREGARD
AT
MANASSAS.

Now glory to the Lord of Hosts, oh, bless and praise His name,
That hath battled in our cause, and brought our foes to shame;
And honor to our BEAUREGARD, who conquered in His might,
And for our children's children, won Manassas' bloody fight.
Oh, let our thankful prayers ascend, our joyous praise resound,
For God, the god of victory, our untried flag hath crowned,

They brought a mighty army to crush us with a blow,
And in their pride they laughed to scorn the men they did not know;
Fair women came to triumph with the heroes of the day,
When the boasting Southern Rebels should be scattered in dismay;
And for their conquering Generals lordly feasts were spread;
But the wine in which we pledged them was all of ruby red.

The feast was like Belshazzar's—in terror and dismay—
Before our conquering heroes their Generals ran away—
God hath weighed them in the balance, and his hand upon the wall
At the taking of Fort Sumter, hath foredoomed them in their fall;
But they would not heed the warning; and scoffed in unbelief,
Till their scorn was turned to wailing, and their laughter into grief.

All day the fight was raging, and amid the cannon's peal,
Rang the crack of our rifles, and the clashing of our steel;
But once our spirits faltered, BEE and BARTOW both were down,
And our gallant COL. HAMPTON lay wounded on the ground,
But BEAUREGARD—God bless him! led the legion in his stead,
And JOHNSTON seized the colors, and waved them o'er his head;
E'en a coward must have followed, when such heroes led the way,
And no damned blood was flowing in Southern veins that day.

Every arm was strengthened and every heart was stirred,
When cheers of DAVIS! DAVIS! along our lines were heard;
As he rode into the battle, the joyous news flew fast;
And the dying raised their voices and cheered him as he passed;
Oh! with such glorious leaders in Cabinet and in field,
The gallant Southern chivalry will die, but never yield!

BEAUREGARD.

*Flashing, flashing along the wires,
The glorious news each heart inspires,
The war in Charleston has begun
Its smoke obscured this morning's sun;
As with cannon, mortar and petard,
We saluted the North with our Beauregard.

See the crowds in every street,
Scan the face of each man you meet,
Hear their purpose in every breath,
Fight to the last, aye fight to the death!
And with cannon, mortar and petard,
Salute them with our Beauregard.

Morris and Pinckney and Johnson too,
And Moultrie filled with the brave and true,
Thousands are hourly rushing in,
Eager to join the battle's din;
To hoist Old Abe with his own petard,
And salute him with our Beauregard.

Ere the sun goes down this April day,
The Palmetto free from Lincoln's sway,
Shall stand as the emblem green and
　strong,
Of the bold brave hearts who atoned her
　wrong,
Who with cannon, mortar and petard,
Avenged the South with Beauregard.

The battle's fought, the victory's won,
†Abe's flags hauled down by Anderson,
Now the Border States no more will retard,
But wheel into line under Beauregard;
And with cannon, mortar and petard,
Take Washington with Beauregard.

‡Another deed heroic's done,
Another blooming chaplet won;
By that peerless dauntless one,
Louisiana's gallant son,
And now no army can retard
Washington's capture by Beauregard.

On Manassas bloody field,
We made the hireling Hessians yield;
And following fast to see the fun,
Forced them back on Arlington;
As with cannon, mortar and petard,
We saluted Old Abe with our Beauregard.

How long for assistance, must we look?
How long must we such insults brook?
The time is coming, aye! soon will come,
When here we'll hear the Old Line's
　drum,
When with cannon, mortar and petard,
They'll free Maryland with Beauregard.

*April 12th, April 14th, July 21st, 1861.

CHAPTER THREE

PUBLIC SENTIMENT REACHED across the pages of newspapers, after Manassas, to hail heroes and vilify enemies. One of the chief heroes was General Pierre G. T. Beauregard. One of the chief enemies was, of course, President of the United States Abraham Lincoln, who, to many Southerners, was the symbol of oppression and evil. Even as poems dedicated with equal fervor to friend and enemy appeared, dissension was growing in Confederate councils. The thin threads of compromise that had held Bob Toombs in the Davis government were severed. Toombs left the cabinet and Robert Hunter of Virginia (below) took his place.

With the wounded flowing back to Richmond from Manassas, the war took on a grim character. The bright uniforms came back no longer bright but dirty and bloodstained, and the men in the uniforms also seemed changed. Still, despite the evident impact of the conflict on all sides, much that was customary in Richmond and other great Southern cities continued on. Entertainments in the social season were virtually as elaborate as before. Of course many of the functions were held for charitable causes or for the amusement of officers of this regiment or that which might be then encamped nearby or passing through. And the girls were as beautiful, their manners as gracious and seemingly carefree as before. Yet there were heart-rending moments when the young lady—sister, sweetheart or wife—would come home, after patriotically entertaining other men at parties, to the empty chair and aching memory of some special dear one off at the front.

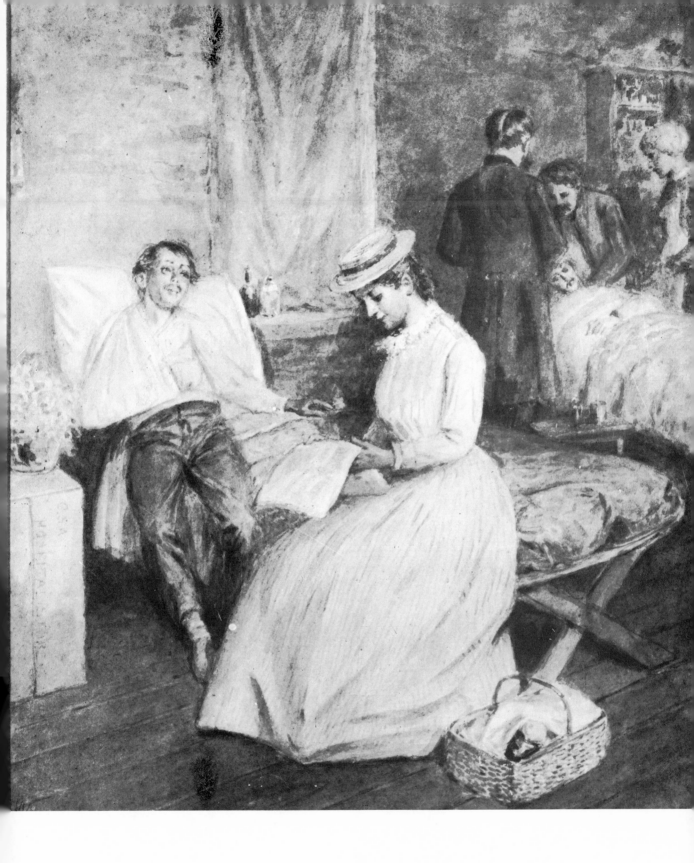

Visits to the hospitals were important, and the Sheppard water color depicts a familiar scene as women brought what they could in the way of cheer and delicacies to tempt the appetites of the ailing.

The Confederacy was recognized as a belligerent by England and France during the early days of the War Between the States, but not as an independent state. Accordingly, James Mason (left above) and John

Slidell (right) were sent to represent the Confederate States in London and Paris. It was long the hope of the Richmond government that foreign intervention on their side might contribute important help to the South. The British mail steamer *Trent*, carrying Mason and Slidell, was intercepted by the Union sloop of war *San Jacinto* (opposite page) and the two Confederate agents taken prisoner, causing immediate commotion in British circles about this "unwarranted search and seizure." Fearful that the episode might precipitate Great Britain into a full-scale, armed alliance with the Confederacy—just what he wished to avoid—Lincoln ordered Mason and Slidell released and eventually they went on to Europe to plead the case of the Confederacy, though with less than hoped-for success.

67

When the Confederate casualties first returned in surprisingly large numbers from the front, frantic efforts were made to find shelter for the wounded. All manner of private and public buildings were converted hastily into makeshift hospitals. Miss Sally Tompkins, below, was one of the most tireless workers among many valorous women who served long hours in the overcrowded places of mercy.

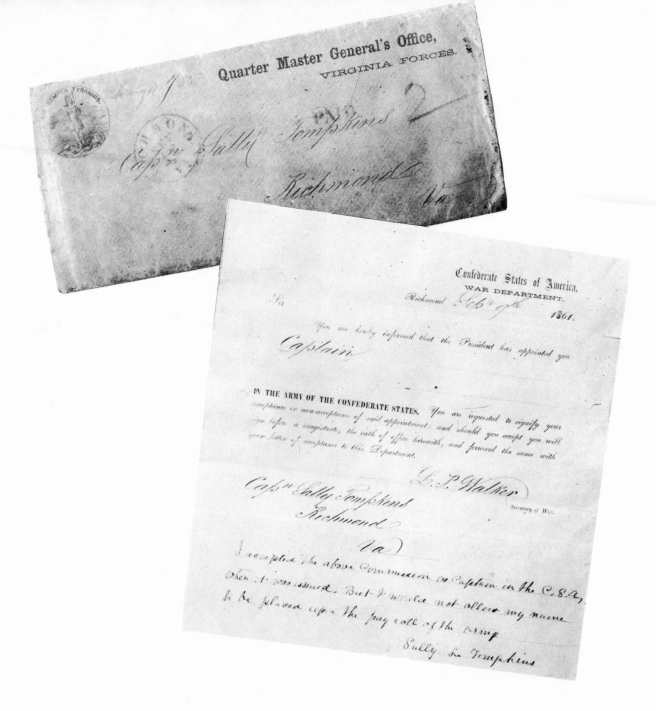

Before long, the authorities made an attempt to rearrange the multitude of lesser hospitals into a few large, well-organized ones. The indispensable workers in these establishments were publicly commended as "soldiers without guns." Among them was Miss Sally Tompkins, who received a commission in the Confederate Army as well as a commendation, the only such commission ever issued to a woman, and a unique "first" for any American army. It is interesting to note the handwritten postscript to the official message to Captain Tompkins from the War Department. She accepted the commission but "would not allow my name to be placed upon the payroll."

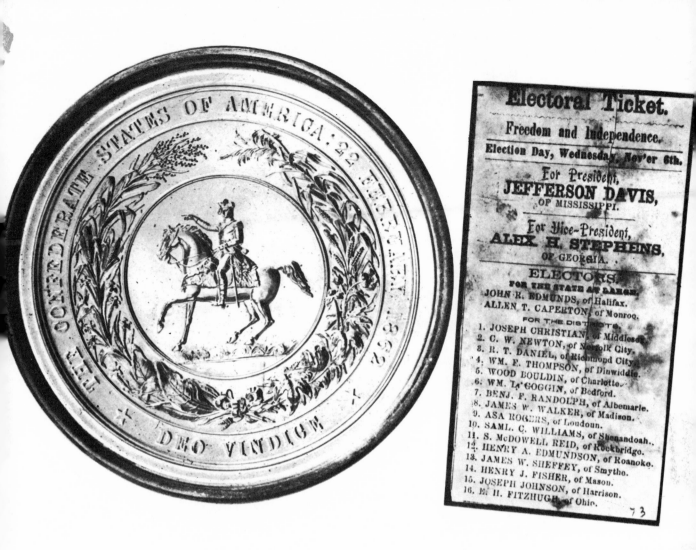

The permanent Congress assembled in Richmond on February 18, 1862. Four days later, while an icy rain swept the streets, Jefferson Davis was inaugurated permanent President. Vice-President Alexander H. Stephens was also on hand, complaining about the miserable weather and his frail health. Near the flag-draped platform on which Davis took the oath of office, a silent George Washington sat his motionless horse in statue, a replica of which was to form the central figure of the impressive but never-used Great Seal of the Confederacy (above). To the right of the Seal is an Electoral Ticket while on the opposite page, below Davis and Stephens, is the White House of the Confederacy.

The Confederate states over which Davis now stood as chief had grown to eleven in number, with Arkansas, North Carolina and Tennessee having adopted acts of secession the previous spring.

The smiling gentleman on the opposite page was one of the busiest office-holders in the Confederate Government. First, Attorney General, then Secretary of War, finally as Secretary of State on to the end of the war, Judah Philip Benjamin of Louisiana was sometimes referred to even by those who were not overly fond of him as the "brains" of the government. His talents lay largely unused in the Attorney General's office, but Benjamin was content to bide his time while other more impatient men were scrabbling for political power and thus, figuratively, losing their heads in the scuffle with those as ambitious. Both an immensely able lawyer and an adroit politician, Benjamin was wealthy and had made his wealth by virtue of the system the South represented. He had no reason to question slavery or the right of the Southern states to secede, though he considered that a last resort. It has been suspected that Benjamin always realized the limitations beyond which fervor and devotion could not carry a cause so handicapped in material resources. Regardless of his private thoughts, Judah Benjamin served well and loyally in all his posts. Between Davis and him there was a bond of affection stemming from the time when, as members of the U. S. Senate, an unimportant argument between them almost led to a duel. Benjamin, who made no secret of his pleasure in good living, was probably little more concerned than his confreres with complaining broadsides, like the one below from "One of the people" complaining that the use of corn for whiskey made it harder for the poor man to buy bread. But he was more likely than they to recognize the underlying causes of which this broadside was but a symptom.

Shall the distiller grow rich and the people starve?

This is an important question—one which must *of necessity* interest the public. The distillers are comparatively few, the *people* many. Shall the few fatten and grow rich while the *many* starve? This is the question which I propose to discuss briefly. The immoral and injurious practice of indulging in the use of ardent spirits, as a beverage, has been ably discussed—it is not my purpose to treat that subject at all in this article—the question has assumed a different aspect, and the *morality* of it is not necessary to be discussed now. It is not *now* a question whether it is hurtful to *drink* whiskey, brandy, &c., but whether the MAKING of these poisons out of the breadstuffs of the country will not bring a famine upon us. One distillery which has come under our observation is *destroying* one thousand bushels of corn (the staff of life) per day. Another four hundred bushels, &c. &c. Suppose we have a short crop next season, what then! If the distillers are allowed to go on, starvation *must* ensue. The distiller can better afford to pay *five* dollars per bushel for corn to make into whiskey, than the poor man can afford to pay *one* dollar for bread. In nine cases out of ten he (the distiller) will become the purchaser of the grain, inasmuch as he *can well afford to pay more than any one else*, because whiskey which he used to sell at from twenty three to thirty cents per gallon he now gets from two dollars and fifty cents to three dollars and fifty cents per gallon. We would rightly consider that man an enemy to the Confederacy and the State, who would buy up all the corn in our county, and taking it to a given point set fire to and burn it. The distiller is engaged in a far more injurious business. Not only does he destroy the corn but he converts it into that which destroys the health and lives of our soldiers, the noble men who are defending us from Yankee invasion and oppression. Shall we condemn the man who would simply destroy the corn, and yet have no word of reproach for the individual who is murdering our brethren? Shame upon us! But perhaps corn burning would be illegal, while distilling it may be urged, is a *legal* business. It would be a monstrous thing to burn the corn, but if one can so fix it as to destroy the corn and the life of his fellow at the same time, (kill two birds with one stone) he is to be accounted a *benefactor* and have the *strong arm of the law* thrown around his nefarious business. Shame upon such a law! If we intend to act in this matter there is no time to be lost: already corn is one dollar per bushel and very soon if the distillation of grain goes on, flour will be $10 to $12 per barrel. Then comes suffering, want, and ere long starvation. Let us send up petition after petition to the Legislature demanding of that body that they shall interpose between us and the distiller. It is a matter to which they cannot close their eyes, or stop their ears, and they *will heed* our petitions. Let us make them understand that these breathing holes of the infernal regions must be closed at least during the war.
ONE OF THE PEOPLE.

WYTHE COUNTY,
February 8th, 1862.

On the military side, General Ben McCulloch was a potent figure at the head of Confederate forces in Arkansas and the Indian Territory. McCulloch had won against Lyon, the peppery commander of the Lindell's Grove episode, this time at Wilson's Creek. A Texan, McCulloch had served under the great Sam Houston. He had commanded a company of Texas Rangers and was an out-of-doors man who knew and understood instinctively the use of terrain as a military ally.

As the anniversary of Fort Sumter approached, President Davis averred that "Events have cast upon our arms and our hopes the gloomiest shadows." But there was worse news to come. In the West, Fort Donelson had been lost, Nashville to follow, and much of Kentucky and Tennessee became indefensible. Early in March, forces under Van Dorn, Price and McCulloch were defeated at Pea Ridge and Confederate operations in Missouri were thwarted. Even as papers were printing eulogies to that "Brave Old Fellow," Ben McCulloch himself was killed in the action. Grant's forces were concentrating around Pittsburg Landing where (above) Union gunboats berthed. The middle steamer, the *Tigress*, was General Grant's headquarters boat. Meanwhile McClellan continued methodically building up his strength and—everybody in the South suspected—planning how best he might attack Richmond.

Despite operations elsewhere, many believed that the key to the war and its duration was Virginia. The North hoped that the spring campaigns there might yield Richmond and thereby end the war. The South devoutly believed that their boys in Confederate gray could blunt any McClellan thrust toward the capital.

The Federal General Ben Butler added a new word to the vocabulary of war. He applied the term contraband not only to property but to the slaves who came within his grasp as well. At top, opposite page, is a photo of a contraband camp in Virginia. It was Butler's belief that slaves "had given or could give aid and comfort to the Confederates" and should, therefore, be treated like any enemy war asset. The woodcut opposite shows "Federal Troops impressing the contraband in Nashville to the obvious discomfort of the slaves who were sometimes un-

pleasantly surprised by the treatment they received from these uniformed representatives of a people publicly pledged to their liberation." Above, a sketch illustrating the "underground" system of transportation which operated all during the war between North and South. Sometimes it was used, as here, to help slaves escape from the South. At other times it was used by smugglers to bring in vital supplies, for the delivery of letters (sometimes as high as two dollars per letter) and for the exchange of information by spies.

The blockade of Southern ports was never so effective as the North boasted, or as ineffective as the Confederates wished. Southerners sometimes spoke about the blockade in much the same manner as they referred to such nuisances as a spell of very bad weather or an unruly child. Many things could be blamed on it; many jokes were based on "Running the Blockade," as above.

In reality, the policing of any port was not easy, having to concern itself with natural difficulties like weather and tide as well as with the enemy. The Confederates became adept at torpedoing or ramming Federal ships and otherwise bedeviling them. The North, in return, executed such maneuvers as the sinking of fifty stone-filled ships—as viewed in this Volck engraving—across the channel at Charleston Harbor. An official British observer termed this "a cruel act," though little

lasting damage was done as the ebb and flow of the tides broke up the sunken vessels.

John H. Reagan, the Postmaster General from Texas, looked as grim working in his office as he did sitting for his portrait. Reagan, who had made a creditable reputation for himself in Texas, assumed the Postmaster General's duties when, as he said, "no one else would take the job." It fell to Reagan to operate the mails in the absence of any established postal system and despite shortages of engravers, die-makers, ink, paper, presses, sealing wax and the technical know-how to turn the total of these into stamps. Considering its extreme disadvantages the postal service did well.

Popular songs told of the hopes and fears, the boasts and true patriotism of the people. From New Orleans and Mobile to Columbia and Richmond, composers of the usual widely varying degrees of talent put the spirit and problems of the times into music and words. One store in Charleston, South Carolina, advertising a new, defiant air with equally defiant words, placed a sign in the window which read: "Lift up your spirits. Come in and be cheered by a sheet of the 'No Surrender' song."

Northern papers now began to editorialize about a new threat to Northern shipping as "Rebel" raiders like the *Nashville* here, specially fitted out to do the job, were set loose on sea commerce.

First cruiser to fly the Confederate flag in European waters, the *Nashville's* most notable achievement probably was slipping the blockade at Beaufort to bring in much-needed military supplies.

If Reagan was appointed to head a non-existent postal service, the somewhat preposterous situation of a Secretary-without-a-Department was no less true for Secretary of the Navy Stephen Russell Mallory, below. For at war's start, there was no Confederate Navy, and there was little knowledge or conviction on the part of most government officials of the important role a navy must play in an area crisscrossed with rivers and bounded on two sides by great water masses. Even President Davis gave little thought to the importance of some sort of water defense of the South. But Mallory, a Floridian who once had said publicly: "I fear the perils of secession," was a man who understood ships and the role they should play. Though the South had less of the seagoing tradition than the North and boasted not one warship at the conflict's start, Mallory immediately set about with vigor to improvise and invent a Navy.

"Men, the eyes of your country are upon you. . . . Go to your guns!" So spoke Commodore Franklin Buchanan to his crew on the *Virginia* as they headed into what the *Southern Illustrated News* of that time called "the greatest naval engagement that ever took place in American waters." Before resigning his United States commission so he might serve the Confederacy, Buchanan, commanding the *Virginia*, had been one of the most distinguished officers of the old Navy, a veteran of forty-five years' service, father of the Naval Academy at Annapolis as well as its first Superintendent. Mallory, believing that he could not match the North ship for ship, stated: "Inequality of numbers may be compensated for by invulnerability," and the ironclad *Virginia*, built from the bones of the old U. S. frigate *Merrimac*, came into being. On March 8th of 1862, the squat, grotesque-looking vessel steamed into Hampton Roads and within several hours' time had destroyed the two big Union frigates, *Congress* and *Cumberland*.

When news of the catastrophe to U. S. ships of war at Newport News reached Washington, there was considerable anxiety. Lincoln immediately called a meeting of his cabinet. The usually optimistic Seward was downcast, shaking his head silently. Stanton was even more inconsolable, predicting darkly that the naval engagement in Hampton Roads "might change the course of the war." Men looked at one another, wondering if at any instant the ugly, black snout of the *Merrimac*, now *Virginia*, might not appear, nosing up the Potomac for a direct attack on the capital. But during the preceding night a Union rival to the *Virginia* was being towed stealthily through the darkness toward Newport News. On the following day, when the Southern ironclad again lumbered out from shelter to terrorize the large Union fleet in the Roads, she was met by an equally strange-looking vessel, *Monitor*, lying low in the water and mounting a round pill box of a turret in the center.

For many hours the battle between the *Virginia* and the *Monitor* continued. Neither vessel could seriously damage its opponent as even the best-directed shots bounced harmlessly off the iron sides of each into the water. A last attempt to ram the *Monitor* failed because of wheezy engines unequal to the task; the Union ship maneuvered into shallow water where the greater draw of the *Virginia* would not permit pursuit, and the Confederate craft finally drew away.

Though neither side could claim victory, it was certain that the outcome was less satisfactory to the South. The North had a large fleet of conventional-type ships in being and now with an ironclad to match, and therefore discount, the South's *Virginia*, the original advantage was reaffirmed. Thus Confederate Navy hopes that their revolutionary vessel would enable them to drive the Union fleet from Hampton Roads and other harbors of the South were dashed.

The *Monitor* became a maddening symbol of frustration to the South. All Mallory's plans had gone for little; cartoonists drew sarcastic versions of inventor John Ericsson's "iron pot," the *Monitor*. About the respective ironclads, naval construction experts of both North and South had wondered how any such craft could ride the seas properly. The *Monitor*, being even lower, chunkier, and heavier in proportion, caused many doubts. "She'll swamp when the first wave hits 'er," the wooden-ship men swore. But Ericsson, the inventor, merely claimed: "No, the waves will carry over her; she will live in the water like a duck."

The task of protecting from seaside several hundred transports and supply ships around McClellan's base at Fortress Monroe, now fell chiefly to the *Monitor*. Anxiously, the reappearance of the *Virginia* was awaited, but the *Virginia* did not come.

WITH THE LOSS of Norfolk two months after the historic naval engagement at Hampton Roads, the Confederates ran the *Virginia* ashore and blew her up. More grievously wounded in her battle with the *Monitor* than had been suspected at the time, the ironclad drew too much to be brought up the river when Southern troops were forced to retreat in that direction. Before this, McClellan had started his siege of Yorktown, while in the West Albert Sidney Johnston and Beauregard were squaring off against Grant and Buell for the fateful days of Shiloh, to mean eventually another disappointment for the South.

The Volck engraving depicts "Albert S. Johnston crossing the desert to join the Southern army." Johnston, a Kentuckian by birth, was another soldier who previously had served the United States in the Army for many years. Aside from his military ability, which was great, Johnston had a largeness of spirit which was often commented on by fellow officers and men alike. By now the Union had thrown many gunboats into the western rivers, and this immediately placed the South at considerable disadvantage, making more precarious communications between the many land areas separated by bodies of water.

"I will water my horse in the Tennessee River or in hell before night," Beauregard had said to his soldiers on the morning before the battle of Pittsburg Landing. When the tide turned against the Confederates, this cartoon illustrated the grim alternative. At first it had seemed that Shiloh would become a Southern victory. Observers reported that even during a charge by General Grant, his soldiers "looked bewildered and confused," below.

THE SAVANNAH REPUBLICAN

—BY F. W. SIMS,

CITY AND COUNTY PRINTER.

JAMES R. SNEED, ... EDITOR.

SAVANNAH, GA.

Monday Morning. April 7, 1862.

EXTRA

IMPORTANT FROM THE
Battle-Field!

THE GREAT BATTLE IN THE WEST!

The Confederates ¡Commence the Action!

A GREAT VICTORY, PROBABLE!

The Battle still Progressing!

[Special Despatch from our Army Correspondent.]

CORINTH, April 6 — It is thought that the great battle of the West is opened. The Confederates have offered battle and heavy firing has been heard at intervals for three hours. Our centre is probably engaged. There was considerable skirmishing yesterday.

The Texas Rangers have taken 50 prisoners, including Major Crockett, of Ohio.

The Confederates are confident of success. It is doubtful whether Buell's column from Nashville has just got into position.

LATER.

CORINTH, April 6.—10 a m.—The great battle commenced at daylight this morning, General Hardee leading the attack. A courier has just arrived, who says that the infantry opened the fight, firing heavily.

The reports of artillery seem more distant; the enemy may be falling back. I am off for the battle field, sixteen miles distant.

Confederates. The battle field is a wooden, broken country, presenting opportunities for a great variety of manoeuvres and independent operations by comparatively small bodies of men.

STILL LATER.

The battle is still raging, fierce and furious. The Confederates are still slowly forcing the enemy back. Our loss is heavy, but our men are in good spirits.— The Alabama, Mississippi and Louisiana troops are showing great gallantry. All, though, fight well. The Twenty-first Alabama Regiment has taken two Federal batteries, and the Louisianians have taken one. Gen. Bushrod Johnson is wounded.

Our reserves have not yet gone into the fight. Our troops are now preparing for a grand charge. We are almost "out of the woods." P. W. A.

Latest News!!

GLORIOUS VICTORY IN THE WEST!

A SECOND MANASSAS!

Large Number of Officers Captured!

General Sidney Johnston Killed!

BEAUREGARD IN COMMAND!

[From our Special Army Correspondent.]

BATTLE FIELD NEAR CORINTH,
April 6, 6 o'clock P. M.

Victory! Victory!! Victory!!!

We have fought a terrible but glorious battle, and the day is ours. The enemy are in full retreat, and our forces are in hot pursuit of them. I write from the enemy's camp and on Federal paper.

A large number of prisoners have, already, been taken, and we expect certainly to capture the greater part of the Federal army. We are driving them back on the river, and if the transports are not convenient, we shall kill and capture the entire army.

The battle is still raging. The earth trembles beneath me from the tremendous cannonade. We are pressing forward with the force of fate. We have captured General Prentiss and a large number of Federal officers.

But alas! alas! General Albert Sidney Johnston is killed. He fell at half-past two o'clock. His leg was torn off by a shell, and a minnie ball struck him in the side. He died leading at the head of his army, and in the very arms of victory.

Gen. Beauregard is in command . . . .

THE BATTLE OF PITTSBURG LANDING!

FULL PARTICULARS!!

GEN. A S JOHNSON KILLED!

GEN. TOM CRITTENDEN. ALSO, REPORTED KILLED!

3,500 Prisoners Taken!

GEN. PRENTISS AMONG THEM!

Special Correspondence of the Memphis Argus.

CORINTH, April 7.

Yesterday morning, (Sunday,) everything having been in readiness, Gen. Hardee moved up his division to within a mile of the enemy's encampments, which extended between Lick and Owl creeks, a distance of six miles, and from Pittsburg landing, on the river, four miles into the interior. At early dawn the column commenced steadily advancing, and before it was yet light were upon the enemy, who were taken completely by surprise, and, being panic stricken, fled towards the river, deserting their camps and leaving behind them all their camp equipage and one battery of light artillery.

This was on the enemy's right, at a place known as Shiloh church. In half an hour after the attack the entire Federal camp was aroused, and their forces, which Federal officers who were taken prisoners estimated at 70,000 men, put under arms. Following Hardee's advance a general movement was made by our line, and by 9 o'clock the battle raged at its height. Steadily our troops commenced advancing, the enemy slowly falling back, desperately disputing every foot of ground.—

At 10 a. m., we had captured three batteries of rifled guns, the gunners and horses being killed and the supporting force of infantry driven back into the woods, hotly pursued by our conquering troops.

At eleven o'clock our generals became satisfied that thus early in the day we had gained a victory, as at all points the enemy were giving away, unable to withstand the terrible charges of our infantry and the numerous . . . of artillery, whi . . . . . scores at all . . . . . . had char . . . . . . cessfully . . .

Shiloh was first hailed by the South, as in the *Savannah Republican*, as "a Great Victory." There was sadness, too. Albert Sidney Johnston had been killed when he disregarded a severe leg wound, fighting on until the loss of blood overcame him. However, as time passed and further word filtered back from the wooded glens and ravines of Shiloh and Corinth, reports, no longer claiming sweeping victory, were content to say that "our loss is heavy but our men are in good spirits" or that the "Twenty-first Alabama Regiment has taken two Federal batteries." Also in action at Shiloh was the Confederate Lieutenant General William J. Hardee, here, whose *Infantry and Rifle Tactics* was the standard work of its kind used by both the Confederate and Union Armies.

By August, 1861, Lincoln had ordered a draft of militiamen. By March of the next year the United States Congress enacted legislation making all able-bodied males, with certain exceptions, liable to military duty. The South, with a much smaller potential of military-age man-power, pushed through a rather unpopular Conscription Act in April of 1862.

On both sides, conscription faced bitter opposition. There were riots protesting the draft in the North, while in the Confederacy bitter denunciations against the law were heard from states'-righters and others who felt that all men who were able and could be spared from the home front would volunteer anyway. Even Vice-President Stephens opposed conscription, and Southern cartoons sometimes poked fun as shown.

Criticism of President Davis and his administration increased with the bad news that filtered back from the fronts. Desertions increased in the Confederate Army, although it is probably true that, as reliable journals of the time stated, they were never "one-half of what the desertion rate was in the Federal armies." It was also pointed out, not without considerable truth, that when a Confederate soldier left his brigade without permission, like as not he wanted to go home to get in the crop or repair the family house. The so-called "factory-worker soldiers and professional Hessians" from the North had no such obligations, according to this view.

Still there were complaints everywhere throughout the South, and some of those came from the men in the ranks. Cries were heard of "Rich man's war and poor man's fight." Recruiting officers met resistance in some places. Folk who did not lack patriotism, nevertheless, became indignant at evidence that their own Government was adopting the very methods which seemed to characterize the enemy.

With internal unrest and arguments growing, there had to be a prison for political recalcitrants and criminals. Castle Thunder (below) in Richmond served this purpose, under the supervision of Provost Marshal Winder, who vigorously upheld law and order and suppressed espionage with the aid of a motley collection of "secret police" who were sometimes more frightening than the evil-doers.

These pictures show the Confederate fortifications at Yorktown, Virginia. It was the hope of soldiers in gray there, of the Richmond government, and of people throughout the South that they might hold fast in the face of McClellan's determined attack which, rumor said, was contrived to sweep every Southern family from its home from Williamsburg to Richmond.

Newspapers in the Northern states were carrying banner headlines hailing the second "On to Richmond" drive which, strategists continually believed, might end the war if successfully carried out. The Confederate Government was already sending certain archives and records to Columbia, South Carolina, and some factions, with one eye on the crumbling defenses of Yorktown, were suggesting the uselessness of defending Richmond. But Lee felt that the capitulation of Richmond would mean the fall of the Confederacy, and soon afterward President Davis announced to a cheering crowd: "Richmond will be defended."

96

This print shows an attack by the 1st and 11th Massachusetts volunteers on Confederate positions in the background near Yorktown in late April. Affairs were going badly for the South at Yorktown as McClellan brought more and more pressure to bear on the defending positions. There was not much fighting at Yorktown. Just as McClellan was preparing to shell the Confederate works with heavy guns, Johnston withdrew to Williamsburg. But any fighting was bitter fighting. Not at all like the neat lithographs and prints which adorned journals of the day. Fighting men rarely, except in the unrealistic imaginations of artists, advanced in neat lines, in step with muskets over the shoulder like soldiers on parade. More often, the men ran or jumped or belly-crawled, cursing as they went, from shrub to stump, dirty, disheveled and sometimes blood-caked. War was then, as before and still, not alone the romantic, pulse-quickening sound of military bands, the sight of brave men in bright uniforms marching against the enemy in precise, confident lines. It was filth and pain and disease; often death for the victors and vanquished alike.

Yorktown was relinquished. In the Mississippi Valley, Beauregard had been driven back, Morgan had run into an unexpected setback in Tennessee; New Orleans and now Pensacola had been evacuated and taken over by United States troops. There was much to cause the Confederate States concern. But for these two stalwarts on horseback, the South was profoundly grateful. Lee was, of course, Lee. A South which had respected him, then come to adore him, now worshiped him. He was a man who grew in stature even as the cause for which he fought became less prosperous. The intensely religious Stonewall Jackson cared little for the glamor and trappings of war but believed in its righteousness with a fierceness that almost frightened those who did not know him. Comparatively, Lee was a gentle man with a mind that could not help seeing both sides of all controversies. Jackson first had to "see the right," then hell's fury could not deter him. Different as these two men were, they got along well, and each had great respect for the other. And when Lee was to hear of the wound to Jackson that later proved fatal, he wrote: "You have lost your left arm, but I have lost my right."

General J. E. B. Stuart, the immortal "Jeb," was the man who popularized the cavalry. Stuart spent many months showing farmers and plowboys and planters' sons how to be good cavalrymen; but the main requirement for joining these mounted ranks still remained the ownership of a horse. Stuart, popular with his men, was also every young Southern belle's idea of what an officer should look like, with his dark reddish hair, his rich beard and steady gaze. He wore high cavalry boots and was fond of a fancy plumed hat which soon caused bystanders to cry, "Here comes Stuart" when they spotted that personal trademark.

"If you want to have a good time, jine the cavalry!" So singing, Jeb Stuart and his men returned from their spectacular reconnaissance around McClellan. Stuart's ride set a pattern in Confederate cavalry raids for the entire war. Southern arms had to make up in vitality, in courage and in daring what they lacked in sheer quantity. Nowhere was this more true than in the cavalry. Sent by Lee to get what information he could about the enemy, audacious Jeb, heading a force of little more than a thousand, galloped around McClellan's flank, occasionally coming within the line of Federal outposts and often within easy musket shot of the enemy forces. When he had reached the Union rear, gathering what information he needed, he promptly set out for home, going around in the other direction and completing the giant circle safely. However, Stuart's ride hurried McClellan's withdrawal of base to the James River, thereby upsetting Lee's plan to attack him.

TO THE
Citizens of the State,
AND THE
PEOPLE of RICHMOND

THE ENEMY UNDOUBTEDLY

ARE APPROACHING THE CITY!

And may be expected at any hour, with a view to its capture, its pillage, and its destruction. The strongest considerations of self and of duty to the country,

CALL EVERY MAN TO ARMS!

A duty which none can refuse without dishonor. All persons, therefore, able to wield a musket, will immediately

Assemble upon the Public Square

Where a regiment will be found in arms, and around which all can rally, and where the requisite directions will be given for arming and equipping those who respond to this call.

☞ The Governor confidently relies that this appeal will not be made in vain.

WM. SMITH,
GOVERNOR OF VIRGINIA.

In May of 1862 General McClellan took time to write to his wife: "I believe the blows the Rebels have received lately ought to break them up." It was felt by many Union people that the South must now be in the early stages of dissolution, and such reckless things as Stuart's raid were merely symptoms of desperation. The head of an inferior army —inferior in numbers, supplies and the material supports of war, though certainly not in willingness and courage—must be ready to take such outrageous chances. By June, Lee was in command of the Army of Northern Virginia, as it came to be called, and in Washington military men told Lincoln: "If there be one man, Confederate or Union, head and shoulders above every other in daring, it is General Lee." Richmond was an armed camp. Bugle calls from encampments around the city could clearly be heard. At night some swore they could see the camp-fires of the enemy brightening the not-so-distant sky. All persons "able to wield a musket" were expected to stand ready for the anticipated onslaught.

The morale of the city was not helped by word from some of the areas now occupied by the Yankees telling of United States commissaries which had been set up there, as above, plentifully supplied with "corn meal, salt fish and hardtack."

General Stuart's daring horsemen were everywhere. It was a popular—though perhaps fictional—story that often even General Lee, who inspired some of the raids, did not always know exactly where Jeb was thundering off to. Certainly the Union forces were completely mystified. Above is a Volck engraving of one of Stuart's spectacular dashes and raids, this to White House, the McClellan base on the Pamunkey, while to the right is a cartoon-illustrated thought from the *Southern Illustrated News* disparaging "The Yankee Cavalry sent to intercept General Stuart."

"I ask for every man that the War Department can send me," George McClellan sent word to Lincoln when earlier requests to Stanton had gone unanswered.

Here was McClellan's base of operations on the Pamunkey. A camp of mud-splattered supply wagons, foraging horses and of soldiers who had been told by their officers that they were about to strike a blow which could bring close the end of the war. General McClellan was less confident of this himself, though. Lee's forces were known to be formidable but of indeterminate numbers. Military intelligence, usually in the hands of such as Allan Pinkerton—the great detective now turned to espionage—and his secret agents, seemed to conflict on the exact size of Southern troop concentrations. McClellan was led to believe that the Confederates had 200,000 men. Actually Lee had less than 100,000 at his disposal. McClellan determined not to move until reinforced by Mc-Dowell. So the anticipated Union drive on Richmond did not then materialize. Instead, the Confederates turned to attack.

There were constant skirmishes between men and detachments from each army. Though many of these have retained no particular historical significance, it was, as a writer in the *Magnolia Weekly* commented: "A matter of great importance wherever and whenever battle is joined, even by one soldier of each side." A casualty, a fatality, was no less a fact because it had been suffered in some lonely struggle between small groups instead of at Frayser's Farm or Gaines' Mill. To a fighting soldier, every piece of contested ground was dear, every river ford was a Rappahannock, every slope a Cemetery Ridge. A man neither knew nor cared whether he was fighting a "great" battle or an unimportant skirmish, for history does not reveal its judgment on these matters in advance.

Mechanicsville (right) was a name on many tongues throughout the South after the Seven Days battle around Richmond. There the two Hills (A. P. and D. H.), attacked Federal troops at Beaver Dam Creek. Above is Malvern Hill, where the closing chapter of the Seven Days took place. Reports that the Federal army had been "defeated and utterly routed" were proved untrue as Lee's brigades charged again and again up the slope commanded by the guns of the Army of the Potomac until the grass was slippery with blood. Confederate casualties were more than five thousand men.

Even as some of the dead were buried not far from where they had fallen at Malvern Hill, as pictured here in the *Southern Illustrated News*, men also died on the side of the North (below). But there always seemed new muskets and fresh recruits to hold them, ready to spring into the ranks. The Confederate States, with a potential military population less than one half of the enemy's, must of necessity use that manpower as sparingly as possible. Nevertheless, spirits were higher than they had

been for some time in July of 1862. People who but short weeks before had felt the depression of knowing that the enemy was less than five miles from Richmond now breathed easier. Lee himself was neither elated nor satisfied. Some military authorities have called Malvern Hill a considerable mistake. Yet when McClellan's army had been thrown into retreat, it appeared that one more coup might well have effected its utter destruction. This was the lure that drove the Confederates on to storm a natural redoubt upon whose heights Union troops were able to gather their forces and wits, saving defeat from becoming utter annihilation and inflicting terrible losses on the attackers. The sweltering heat which had endured through the Seven Days lifted after Malvern Hill and cooling rain fell, as though to give succor to the wounded, brought back now to Richmond in a seemingly endless train of wagons. Observers who had glimpsed the gigantic rescue operation commented on "the strange sounds of agony, the chants of pain" coming from the mercy vehicles as the procession wound along muddy roads. Back in Richmond, still congratulating itself over the lifting of the siege, people were quickly sobered by the spectacle of wounded everywhere, the appalling number of funerals and the tearstained faces of the bereaved. Sometime later, a soldier at Stonewall Jackson's position north of the Warrenton Pike, near Groveton, pictured below, wrote, "The sky looks so blue, the countryside so green and peaceful, it seems strange to think of the great War that is here."

The summer of 1862 had been a promising one for Confederate arms. After the Seven Days, Richmond was free from the sound of cannonading and its citizens took time to stop in the streets, smile at one another and inquire about the little intimate neighborhood matters that had all but been forgotten during the time of the siege. Jefferson Davis was in better spirits; his wife Varina told friends that the President "has a better appetite and is less exhausted." The brilliant Judah Benjamin was now Secretary of State, and even matters in the Government, at least temporarily,

seemed more harmonious. People on the home front chattered excitedly about all the news, one interesting piece of which concerned the Confederate thrust at Pope's railroad line at Bristoe Station where locomotives and rolling stock were taken. More supplies were captured from the Union base at Manassas Junction (opposite) further north along the tracks, after which the place was fired. Again Southern troops were pursuing Federal soldiers through the mutilated countryside and across the now partially ruined Stone Bridge over Bull Run.

113

"I'm sent to warn the neighbors, he's only a mile behind,
He's sweeping up the horses, every horse that he can find,
Morgan, Morgan the raider, and Morgan's terrible men,
With bowie-knives and pistols are galloping up the glen."

This was the "compliment" put to verse and song, a frightened and astonished countryside paid to John H. Morgan, the famous "raider." Some of the typical consternation caused by such raids is shown above as excited citizens of Covington gather on hearing of Morgan's capture of nearby Cynthiana. Morgan, a Kentuckian, was the enthusiastic instrument of Jefferson Davis' hope of starting a general uprising in Kentucky against the Federal Government. Next to the Morgan proclamation to this end (below) is a somewhat romantic painting of one of Morgan's riflemen, in reality a rough and ready warrior at home in fields and forests, able to live off the land, to move fast and strike hard.

KENTUCKIANS!

I come to liberate you from the despotism of a tyrannical faction and to rescue my native State from the hand of your oppressors. Everywhere the cowardly foe has fled from my avenging arms. My brave army is stigmatized as a band of guerrillas and marauders. Believe it not. I point with pride to their deeds as a refutation to this foul aspersion. We come not to molest peaceful individuals or to destroy private property, but guarantee absolute protection to all who are not in arms against us. We ask only to meet the hireling legions of Lincoln. The eyes of your brethren of the South are upon you. Your gallant fellow citizens are flocking to our standard. Our armies are rapidly advancing to your protection. Then greet them with the willing hands of fifty thousand of Kentucky's brave. Their advance is already with you. Then

"STRIKE FOR THE GREEN GRAVES OF YOUR SIRES!"
"STRIKE FOR YOUR ALTARS AND YOUR FIRES!!"
GOD, AND YOUR NATIVE LAND"
JOHN H. MORGAN,
Brig. Gen. C. S. A.
GEORGETOWN, Ky. July 15th 1862.

Culpeper, another spot of pretty Virginia now dotted with the signs and sounds of armed men bent on the destruction of other men. Below, Wade Hampton, sportsman and wealthy planter from South Carolina, organizer of the famous Hampton Legion, which, with its giant leader, was to fight with high honor. Rumor had it that a new Federal concentration already was building up under Pope at Culpeper and

again Richmond saw the tired, slogging columns of the Army of Northern Virginia shifting to meet the expected blow.

Here are Confederate military commanders and the Chief of Government, varying temperaments united to fight for the South's cause. They are Admiral Semmes, General Hood, President Davis, and Generals Stuart, Jackson, Lee, Forrest, Joseph Johnston and Beauregard. On the wall, at right, is a picture of one general who would fight no more, gallant Albert Sidney Johnston.

Even some of the most vitriolic in the North had respect and downright admiration for Robert E. Lee. Accordingly, his image would turn up regularly in Northern journals, underlined "The Rebel General," in some such pose as holding his field glass in one hand while resting the other on his sword. In his middle fifties when war broke out, Lee, just under six feet in height, made a fine appearance and carried with him wherever he went what was described as "an aura of grandeur." Lee once remarked modestly to a worshipful attendant that he felt he was only as good as the generals with whom he could surround himself. One general, Braxton Bragg (above), helped make the summer of 1862 a cheerful one for the Confederacy with his Kentucky campaign, his capture of Munfordville and threat to Louisville.

--≡{ CHAPTER FIVE }≡--

Christopher Memminger (opposite) was a South Carolinian with a stern manner that sometimes turned his clerks speechless. It was no wonder that Memminger was grim. At the beginning his Treasury Department had no coins or mint, no money certificates or the engravings from which to print them. The first Confederate bills were actually printed in New York, though this fact was not acknowledged on the currency itself. Worse, his department, its policies and, in fact, the money standards of the whole Confederacy were suspect in varying degrees across the Southern states.

At times, to prevent a breakdown of all trade and commerce with the resultant chaos, it was necessary to issue impressive-sounding General Orders maintaining that "the money issued by the Confederate Government is secure."

Despite the well-known handicaps and limitations under which the Treasury and other government departments had to operate, considerable fun was poked at officials, in this case Mr. Memminger, and his monetary policy. And yet this policy was shaped largely by the strengths and weaknesses of the economy of the young nation. Not commanding

the North's plentiful gold and silver supply, Memminger merely did the best he could. The Confederacy, with little hard money anyway, exported a large portion of what it had to buy military supplies. The states were called on for quotas of money to be raised by direct taxes on property. Confederate bonds were exchanged for specie, produce, and state and Confederate notes. Altogether, about $1,000,000,000 worth of paper currency was issued, in addition to notes floated by the states, towns, banks, and business concerns.

GENERAL ORDER.

HEAD QUARTERS,
DEPARTMENT OF WESTERN VIRGINIA,
Charleston, Va., Sept. 24, 1862.

General Order, No.

The money issued by the Confederate Government is secure, and is receivable in payment of public dues, and convertible into 8 per cent. bonds. Citizens owe it to the country to receive it in trade; and it will therefore be regarded as good in payment for supplies purchased for the army.

Persons engaged in trade are invited to resume their business and open their stores.

By order of   MAJ. GEN. LORING.

H. FITZHUGH,
Chief of Staff.

The Confederate soldier by now bore no surface resemblance to the warrior of many months ago who had gone gladly, even gaily, to serve the Southern cause. Rough uniforms of butternut-colored homespun soon became shabby and torn through continuous usage and constant patching. The photo opposite of a Union Army camp, with soldiers sewing and mending their clothing, as well as writing letters home, was typical in many ways of both sides. Yet, with the Union, the full supply carts, although often outsped by the movement of troops in the field, were never far away. And if a Massachusetts or Connecticut soldier needed a new uniform, the chances were he would be supplied with one. If a soldier of the Texas Brigade or the Third Alabama needed a new uniform, the chances were he would not get it.

There was a story in the South of the rookie asking how he could get himself a new pair of shoes from CSA supply. "If you want a new pair o' shoes, kill yourself a Yankee," was a veteran fighter's reply. It was largely true; the Confederates equipped themselves as much as possible by the seizure of enemy matériel. A Confederate sentry had to be careful after his side raided U. S. supplies, for sometimes a Southern brigade would return in Union trappings, the first new clothing they'd had in many months.

The Southern states had long regarded Maryland as rightfully belonging to their confederation, prevented from acting as that state—or the majority of its citizens—would wish by strong "supervision" from Washington, which needed the area under the U. S. flag for protection of the District of Columbia.

Early in September Stonewall Jackson's divisions marched to the
shores of the Potomac near Leesburg. The men looked across the water
at this narrow point and those who had boots pulled them off. As the
soldiers began to wade across, first one and then another picked up the
chorus of "Maryland, My Maryland" until that rollicking song was
thundering out spontaneously from many throats.

There were conflicting reports as to how the Confederates were received in Maryland. Two Union versions (opposite); from *Leslie's,* the "daughters of Maryland receiving the sons of the North as they marched against the rebel invaders." Another pictured the apocryphal episode of Barbara Frietchie defiantly waving an American flag out of a window in Frederick City. At right, a "female Rebel" in Baltimore. Jackson's troops were greeted happily by many Marylanders, with hostility by some. Lee had already proclaimed that his army came as liberators. Yet there was not the hoped-for rush to enroll in Confederate ranks. Above is ancient Burnside's Bridge fording Antietam Creek, across which McClellan threw his left wing during the battle of Sharpsburg (or Antietam), one of the costliest single day's fighting of the war. The signal tower overlooking Antietam is at right. From this perch the approach of alien troops could be spotted.

Sharpsburg was a calculated risk taken knowingly by Lee, for the possible rewards of success, politically as well as militarily, would have been tremendous. With Jackson at Harper's Ferry, Lee stood before the advancing Army of the Potomac overwhelmingly outnumbered. Yet General Lee knew this McClellan he faced. And despite vastly superior numbers, McClellan could be counted on to act with caution. Again and again the Union commander failed to push forward when it seemed that his probing columns might break through the comparatively thin ranks facing them. For long, McClellan seemed unwilling to throw in his reserves but some experts feel that McClellan is too harshly criticized for this apparent shortcoming. At the time, two of his corps were disorganized and part of his army dispersed. Finally, at the end of day, Federal forces drove forward. And by nightfall more fresh reinforcements from Washington were reaching the Union general.

In these months it was Washington's turn to know consternation and panic. Great guns were hauled through the streets for defense, and the resounding noises of marching men, of mules and horses pulling artillery and supply wagons carried clearly in the crisp September air. The South was expectant; a capital was threatened, but this time it was not their Richmond; it was the enemy's Washington. People tried to imagine how Lincoln, his cabinet and his military advisers felt "with Davis coming to take the President's chair."

OLD
ABE'S LAMENT.

Tune—" The Campbells are Coming."

Jeff Davis is coming, Oh! dear, Oh! dear,
Jeff Davis is coming, Oh! dear;
I dare not stir out for I feel very queer,
Jeff Davis is coming, Oh! dear.

I fain would go home without shedding a tear
About Davis in taking the president's chair;
But I dare not attempt it, Oh! dear, Oh! dear,
I'm afraid he will "hang" me, Oh! dear.

I tried to deceive them, Oh! dear, Oh! dear,
How hard I did strive, Oh! dear;
But it was of no use, as it seems very clear,
Now that Davis is coming, Oh! dear.

Then I tried to coerce them, Oh! dear, Oh! dear,
With thousands of troops far and near;
But they joined me for bread, not for "Union" I fear,
And they hate me the worse, Oh! dear,

Then I tried to blockade them, Oh! dear, Oh! dear,
With a fleet true and steady, Oh! dear;
But England says No! and is coming 'tis clear,
For it is not "effective," Oh! dear, Oh! dear.

I would renounce all the honours, Oh! dear, Oh! dear,
And try to get home as I came,
But I dare not stir out for I feel very queer,
For Davis is coming, Oh! dear.

At the other end of the Southern nation, the barometer of military fortunes had declined. The *Southern Illustrated News* showed a picture of Major General Mansfield Lovell, a West Pointer and native of the District of Columbia, who had been in the news as commander at New Orleans. In April, Farragut's ships and mortar-boats arrived in front of that city and Lovell, with little to offer in the way of defense, retired rather than risk the destruction of New Orleans.

Since occupation of that place, it was known throughout the South that "the fair ladies of New Orleans—the mothers, wives and sisters of our brave soldiers—have repeatedly been grossly insulted by that miserable old wretch, Beast Butler. . . ."

General Benjamin F. Butler, in charge of forces garrisoning the city, had issued the notorious "General Orders, N. 28," retaliating for what he and his officers felt were "slights" to their men by the ladies of New Orleans. Butler's order was reprinted all over the South, headlined as an "outrage" to Southern womanhood; it even provided a Confederate battle cry, "Men, remember Butler!"

BUTLER'S PROCLAMATION.

His outrageous insult to the Women of New Orleans!

Southern Men, avenge their wrongs !!!

Head-Quarters, Department of the Gulf, New Orleans, May 15, 1862.

General Orders, No. 28.

As the Officers and Soldiers of the United States have been subject to repeated insults from the women calling themselves ladies of New Orleans, in return for the most scrupulous non-interference and courtesy on our part, it is ordered that hereafter when any Female shall, by word, gesture, or movement, insult or show contempt for any officer or soldier of the United States, she shall be regarded and held liable to be treated as a woman of the town plying her avocation.

By command of Maj.-Gen. BUTLER,

GEORGE C. STRONG,

A. A. G. Chief of Stables.

The depictions of Benjamin Butler became more uncomplimentary, as in the cartoon above showing him as an animal with an only somewhat human head. Poems inspired by Butler's New Orleans actions on occasion grew too vividly abusive to print; this milder one refers to him as "the vilest of scum," for his "base and dishonorable allegations and intimations against the noble women of New Orleans."

The matter of General Butler's insult was just another example, so those beneath the Mason-Dixon line felt, of the basic failure or inability of Northerners to understand the South. If the women of New Orleans did not wish to fraternize with Federal occupation troops, was that not their right? Southerners further pointed to the slave issue. Northerners still looked upon themselves as the potential liberators of some three million slaves. But in actuality, many of the slaves did not wish to be freed. There were numerous cases of slaves, caught in the no-man's land between advancing and retreating armies, choosing voluntarily to follow their owner-families rather than escape within the lines of the emancipated North. There was a fund of other instances, every Southerner could relate, of searching Union soldiers being thwarted by faithful "Mammies," while all the time "De Massa" hid behind the door.

FREEDOM TO SLAVES!

Whereas, the President of the United States did, on the first day of the present month issue his *Proclamation* declaring "that, *all persons held as Slaves in certain designated States, and parts of States, are, and henceforward shall be free,*" and that the Executive Government of the United States, including the Military and naval authorities thereof, would recognize and

The Proclamation of Emancipation was the most celebrated of all Lincoln's war measures. At war's outbreak many in the North had urged such a move, rolling monster petitions signed by thousands into Washington. But Lincoln hesitated for fear of losing those slave states still in the Union. He was aware of divisions on the abolitionist question in his own camp. He was also aware that such an emancipation was meaningless unless accompanied by victory on the field of war. As late as summer of 1862 Lincoln had written: "If I could save the Union, without freeing any slaves, I would do it."

But in September, encouraged by the result at Antietam Creek, Lincoln warned the secessionist states that unless they returned immediately to the Union, he would deliver a blow directly at the institution of slavery.

When the new year of 1863 came, Abraham Lincoln had fulfilled his promise. In actuality, the Proclamation freed no slaves at all. In those slave states which had remained loyal to the Union, slaves still remained slaves, and so they did in the Confederate states. But certainly the Proclamation electrified the imagination of many people. It supplied a simple slogan to the war, and was indeed a move toward the abolition of slavery throughout the United States.

Throughout the South the opinions of the people were reflected by their cartoonists, who now referred to the post-Proclamation Lincoln as "King Abraham" or "Master Abraham."

HEAD QUARTERS,
ARMY OF KENTUCKY, Sept. 4, 1862.

OATHS OF ALLEGIANCE have been co-erced from the citizens of Kentucky by the Government of the United States, binding such citizens to oppose in all respects the Government of the Confederate States.

Such Oaths will not be respected as of binding obligation by the Major General Commanding the Forces of the Confederate States, and he will sustain and protect all citizens, by every proper means, in the non-performance of such forced oath. They are neither binding in law or conscience.

By command of
Maj. Gen. E. KIRBY SMITH.
GEORGE WM. BRENT,
Lt. Col. & Inspector General.

To the People of Western Virginia.

The Army of the Confederate States has come among you to expel the enemy, to rescue the people from the despotism of the counterfeit State Government imposed on you by Northern bayonets, and to restore the country once more to its natural allegiance to the State. We fight for peace and the possession of our own territory. We do not intend to punish those who remain at home as quiet citizens in obedience to the laws of the land, and to all such clemency and amnesty are declared; but those who persist in adhering to the cause of the public enemy, and the pretended State Government he has erected at Wheeling, will be dealt with as their obstinate treachery deserves.

When the liberal policy of the Confederate Government shall be introduced and made known to the people, who have so long experienced the wanton misrule of the invader, the Commanding General expects the people heartily to sustain it not only as a duty, but as a deliverance from their taskmasters and usurpers. Indeed, he already recognizes in the cordial welcome which the people everywhere give to the Army, a happy indication of their attachment to their true and lawful Government.

Until the proper authorities shall order otherwise, and in the absence of municipal law and its customary ministers, Martial Law will be administered by the Army and the Provost Marshals. Private rights and property will be respected, violence will be repressed, and order promoted, and all the private property used by the Army will be paid for.

The Commanding General appeals to all good citizens to aid him in these objects, and to all able-bodied men to join his army to defend the sanctities of religion and virtue, home, territory, honor, and law, which are invaded and violated by an unscrupulous enemy, whom an indignant and united people are now about to chastise on his own soil.

The Government expects an immediate and enthusiastic response to this call. Your country has been reclaimed for you from the enemy by soldiers, many of whom are from distant parts of the State, and the Confederacy; and you will prove unworthy to possess so beautiful and fruitful a land, if you do not now rise to retain and defend it. The oaths which the invader imposed upon you are void. They are immoral attempts to restrain you from your duty to your State and Government. They do not exempt you from the obligation to support your Government and to serve in the Army; and if such persons are taken as prisoners of war, the Confederate Government guarantees to them the humane treatment of the usages of war.

By command of
MAJ. GEN. LORING.
H. FITZHUGH.
Chief of Staff.

HEAD QUARTERS, DEPARTMENT OF WESTERN VIRGINIA.
CHARLESTON, VA., September 14, 1862.

General Order No.

The Commanding General congratulates the Army on the brilliant march from the Southwest to this place in one week, and on its successive victories over the enemy at Fayette C. H., Cotton Hill, and Charleston. It will be memorable in history, that overcoming the mountains and the enemy in one week, you have established the laws, and carried

When two separate areas, formerly one whole, divide to fight each other, there must be always the dissatisfied and dissident left behind the lines on both sides. The South never gave up hope for some of the Border States. People of Kentucky were told that the oaths which had been "co-erced" from them to support the United States and oppose the Confederacy were binding neither in law nor conscience. In other posted declarations, the people of Western Virginia—Virginians refused for a long time to call it West Virginia; to them it was merely the western part of their state—were urged to help the Confederate Army reincorporate the territory with Virginia and the South.

Hungry men, men in need of everything from food to shoes, from arms and ammunition to mounts, will take what they can get. Plundering, of course, was by no means confined to one side, and in fact, many believe it was more generally carried on by the Union soldiers than by the Confederates. But the Confederates did have the greater need and the least prospect of succor from their own side. Many soldiers in gray had fabulous visions of Yankee supply, consisting of long columns of butchers and chefs with inexhaustible quantities of foodstuffs. The North knew it was not that good; still the Federal commissariats were usually well supplied, and one neutral observer, an Englishman, asked for his comparisons, reported: "You see many more half-starved men in the Confederate States' armies."

GENERAL ORDER.

HEAD QUARTERS,
DEPARTMENT OF WESTERN VIRGINIA,
Charleston, Va., Sept. 15, 1862.

General Order, No.

All public stores, horses, wagons, and property of every description captured by the Army, or in possession of private citizens, will be handed over to the Quarter Master. All plundering of such property will be severely punished. The Commanding General learns that great waste has occurred by want of attention to the law in this respect, and by appropriation of such property in the Army.

By order of   MAJ. GEN. LORING.
                                  H. FITZHUGH.
                                  Chief of Staff.

From the picturesque headquarters spot of Stafford Heights (opposite, top) overlooking the Rappahannock and Fredericksburg, Major General Ambrose Burnside was to launch his attack against Lee's well-disposed forces across the river. A portion of Burnside's artillery at Fredericksburg is shown in a famous photograph by Mathew Brady. The Union general, who had recently taken over command of these forces from McClellan, had more than three hundred cannon, some of the heaviest calibre. General Lee, besides having about one-third less men than Burnside, also was at a disadvantage in the number of artillery pieces. And his need for additional ammunition was so great that the last reserve supply was hurried to him from Richmond. Meanwhile, the Rappahannock flowed somberly by, holding apart two waiting armies, the giant wheels of its river's-edge mills turning ever more slowly in water thickened by December's cold, reminding men eager to fight that there was not much more time to do it in.

There were many sagas of great gallantry and high courage coming
out of Fredericksburg and the Confederate victory there. One of the
most intriguing tales to capture public imagination concerned Barksdale's
Brigade of Mississippi. Two companies were ensconced on the very edge
of a bluff overlooking the site of the old railroad bridge when, in the
moonlight, they saw Federal soldiers working feverishly on a pontoon
bridge intended to stretch from the Stafford shore across the river. When
the pontoon work had been nearly completed to the bank held by the

Confederates, the Mississippians laid down a withering fire on the bridge and its builders, forcing them to retreat along the narrow floats to the opposite side. Soon from that shore came answering blasts of shell, grape and musketry, raking the positions of the Southern marksmen. But every time the Yankees again ventured out onto the river to complete their work, feeling safe after their barrage, the Mississippi sharpshooters would pop up from cover and recommence peppering the ranks of the pontooniers.

Under saturating fire the Mississippians were finally dislodged. Federal construction crews went on with the work, the bridge was finally completed and the Union forces began to ford the river, but only at considerable loss and after a delay which reportedly irked Burnside and Sumner. Meantime, until the pontoons and boards to go upon them could be got into place, the U. S. soldiers came across in boats, barges and anything that would float.

The next day as Union forces were across the river in strength the Confederates withdrew. Burnside's troops, maneuvering on a fog-bound plain, had the Rappahannock at their back and the bristling heights held by the Confederates before them. An attack on such formidable positions seemed suicidal, but Burnside was to order it, and a Union officer, writing afterward to his sister, reported that of every ten men who charged at one hill strongly held by "Johnny Reb" but one reached the top unscathed.

Attack after attack was made by the Federal troops, only to be beaten off with terrible losses. Confederate guns held the strategic positions that the men in blue had to take, and to take those positions the Federals had to cross a terrain made deadly by sweeping, swiveling artillery and small arms fire. The main engagement at Fredericksburg, often called one of the first "modern" battles, took place at Marye's Hill, at the foot of which was the famous stone wall; a severe military obstacle for Union strategists, a slaughter ground for Union soldiers.

A view of the disaster as the Union saw it is revealed in this Currier and Ives print. The legend admits the defeat of the Union Army but insists that "The soldiers of the North are still as ready to meet the Traitors of the South. . . ." A paper in the North asked, "Does this demonstrate the improvement Burnside is supposed to be over McClellan?" while an-

other wondered incredulously how "the best equipped force in the world could be whipped by a batch of Southern ragamuffins!" Happily for himself and his side the "ragamuffin" Confederate soldier had developed a fine knack of being able to exist on less than other soldiers from the standpoint of food, clothing, shelter and comfort, with no impairment in his splendid fighting ability. Union military men on the field paid him that compliment even if some Northern newspaper editors did not. Below, the stone wall where Thomas Cobb's forces stood firm as Union dead piled grotesquely, trying to win the precious ground. At the end, Cobb, a lawyer dedicated to his native state of Georgia and its right to defend itself against the "meddlesome Northerners," fell at the stone wall, mortally wounded. But he lived long enough to know that Burnside had been turned back and the battle won by the South.

Finally the once magnificent army of Burnside had slipped away
across the river in the darkness, leaving behind many of its dead, who
soon became stiffly frozen in the icy air, some propped up in grisly imita-
tion of an outpost line. The North was appalled by the loss, and the *New
York Times* said: "God help us." The plain before the river bank and
the slopes beneath Marye's Heights were areas of complete destruction
for men, animals, and the hopes of Union arms this day. So great had
been the carnage that soldiers were often left to lie where they had fallen
by comrades who had to look to other vital objectives before tending the
casualties. If the wounded were injured too severely to care for themselves, they ran the risk of freezing as nightfall came. Sharpshooters on
both sides remained active even after the heaviest fighting subsided. No-
body dared chance a fire, fearing it might be seen by some keen-eyed
enemy rifleman, and the December night after Fredericksburg's greatest
battle was very cold. The next day there was some sun, but critically
hurt men and animals who had lain out during the dark hours were beyond help.

Many a man fell, to lie forever where he had fallen, the last terrible experience of war frozen forever into his face, his own rifle atop him, and perhaps with only the broken firearm of a comrade near to keep him company. A dead soldier no longer knows a regiment or a brigade or an army. No matter how fervently he has pursued one cause to the end, in death he is neither Confederate nor Union.

⸺⟨ CHAPTER SIX ⟩⸺

WAR INJURIES WERE matters of grave concern to both sides. The passage of shot into or through the body more often than not meant an invitation to infection, and gangrene might next set in. The smell of rotting flesh was commonplace in hospitals, and as there were no magic drugs to curb infections and putrefaction the mortality rate from amputations and all surgery was high.

But there were remarkable cures, too. The man on crutches illustrates some successful surgery enthusiastically discussed in the *Confederate States Medical and Surgical Journal*. The medical feat accomplished was a resection of the hip joint, and the *Journal* commented that this interesting achievement and its subject, "an athletic young soldier," would long be a topic for consideration. An association of Army and Navy surgeons met regularly to debate the various effects of such things as the use of water dressing in gunshot wounds and exchange other information. Questionnaires often were put to members, and in all can be noted the emphasis on battlefront injuries.

From *A Manual of Military Surgery*, prepared for the use of the Confederate States Army, the latest recommended techniques of amputation as illustrated and approved by the Surgeon General's office are shown on the opposite page.

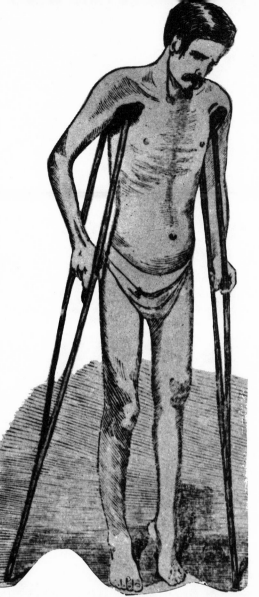

Association of Army and Navy Surgeons.

Richmond, _October 3_ 1863

SIR:

In replying to questions, and in Essays or Papers sent to the Association, a _résumé_ is requested, coming to some conclusion, in order to facilitate taking the vote in the decision on the subject.

THE FOLLOWING QUESTIONS ARE PROPOSED:

I. Any DEATH _from Chloroform in_ YOUR _practice; give particulars of the case, if any. Is this agent always used?_

II. 1st. _Does_ "SHOCK" _postpone_ YOUR _surgical interference; at what period of time, after injury, are_ YOU _usually able to operate?_

    2d. _Any relation between the_ CHARACTER _of the injury, and the_ GRAVITY _of the shock?_

    3d. _Any death, in_ YOUR _practice, from shock_ ALONE?

III. _Do_ CICATRICES _from Gun-shot wounds furnish_ YOU _information as to the nature of the missile which caused the injury, and the probable_ ENTRANCE _and_ EXIT _of the same?_

Further particulars on these subjects, with accounts of any remarkable _course_ which balls may have taken in transit through the body, in _your_ own practice, are solicited.

SAM'L P. MOORE,
Pres't Ass'n A & N. Surgeons.

Address: _Surg._ MIDDLETON MICHEL,
Act. Cor. Secretary,
Box No. 6, Richmond, Va.

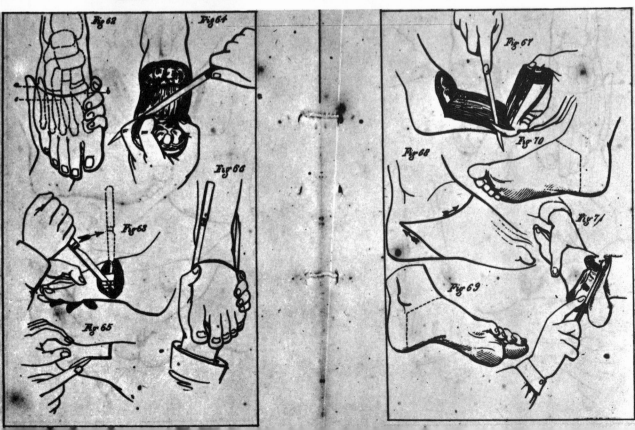

Raphael Semmes (opposite) was, like Buchanan, an officer of the
old Navy who had chosen to follow his state and offer his services to the
Confederacy when the Union split asunder. His first raider was the
Sumter; with it he captured eighteen merchantmen. Later Semmes commanded the *Alabama,* most famous of all Confederate raiders. She was
little more than a thousand tons, about two hundred and fifteen feet
long, barque-rigged, with plenty of canvas and engines that could boost
her sailing speed by a couple of knots. The *Alabama* was both outfitted
into a man of war and commissioned on the high seas. Semmes was a
brilliant captain who knew all the tricks of the sea lanes. One of them
was to burn a prize vessel (above), thus attracting unwary vessels within
range of the *Alabama's* guns.

War was not all bloodshed, agony and privation, and soldiers were not always struggling in the mud or freezing in the snow. In the upper South "winter quarters" meant some relaxation from the main occupation of killing, or being killed. There were the usual drills and formations, roll-call, inspections and picket duty. But in winter quarters, where huts often replaced tents (below), between the bugler's "Reveilles" and dark, there was time for thoughts of home, for gossip, cards and other games. Even the "fights" were more gentle; although snowball warfare between brigades occasionally grew so ferocious that higher-ups had to call the whole thing off.

In Richmond, despite intense shortages, there were dinners and receptions. Many of these were attended by the President and his dark-haired wife (opposite) who was considered a gracious and facile hostess. Davis himself was often "short-tempered, distracted," and it was known that his health was not of the best. And there was much to worry Davis. Faced with the prime necessity of feeding the soldiers, the Government sometimes seized flour that had been earmarked for home-front use. The poor may have had trouble getting bread, but handsome silver service and damask still decorated the well-loaded dinner tables of officials and people of influence.

Steps were taken to prepare the rising generation for the future with new spelling and geography books "adapted to the present condition of the world." As money declined in value, goods of almost all kinds, particularly clothing, became scarce. The child's cloak, illustrated, was an attempt to start fashions "independent of the New York dictation"; this juvenile costume was made of Confederate gray cloth, trimmed in braid and velvet buttons.

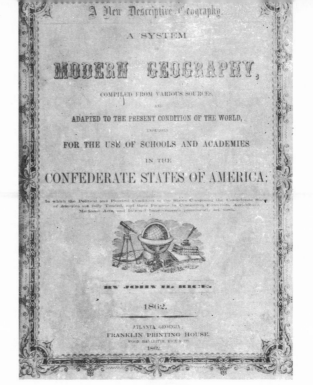

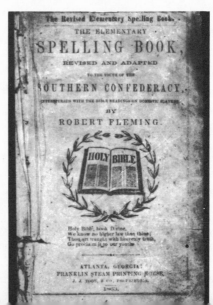

155

The urgent need for supplies sometimes dictated audacious raids by Confederate squadrons. General Nathan Forrest, a serious, brooding man, with an instinct for war though he had little of the formal training received by most of his brother officers, launched a daring attack on Grant's rail communications at Jackson, Tennessee. Forrest, who ordered his men to "charge both ways" whenever surrounded by the enemy, did such a good job tearing up track, burning trestles and taking whatever could be captured, that the railroad was useless for some time.

The railroad raid was a time-honored maneuver. The Confederates liked to swoop down on some section of the United States Military RR, get themselves one of the locomotives and go high-balling down the line creating what havoc they could. With a wood-burning engine it was a pet stunt to fire logs and throw them onto the tracks. This certainly delayed, if not derailed, pursuers. Another expedient in the process of "railroad destruction" was the cutting of telegraph wires, as here illustrated by Stuart's cavalry, effectively preventing those in the rear from signaling warnings ahead.

Fabulous chases involving famous locomotives like the *General* and the *Texas* are among the most exciting escapades of the war. But any Iron Horse was valuable; even more so than his flesh-and-blood namesake. For what stallion could take an artillery shell through his neck (or funnel!) like the iron critter above, and still live to fetch supplies to Hood?

"Morgan, Morgan the raider," and his staff, off across the countryside to do the enemy mischief. Watching such antics, the foot soldier argued that the cavalryman was wedded, if not positively welded, to his

horse and would not dismount under any circumstance. And the man
whose locomotion was his own two legs had some legitimate cause for
complaint. If it came to getting down off their horses to lay explosive
charges or rip up tracks, it seemed many cavalrymen often preferred to
let someone else do it. Not so the "superior" cavalry of Morgan, Stuart
and Forrest. They acted as cavalry but also as infantry when necessary.
And they worked and fought standing, sitting, running or riding with
equal enthusiasm.

General Joseph E. Johnston, left, hears a word from Lee. Johnston's headquarters were at Chattanooga; his command included everything between the mountains and the Mississippi. Old Joe, so-called affectionately by some of the men who had served under him at Seven Pines, took over a modest force comprising Bragg's and Pemberton's troops. Johnston was dubious of his position from the first and did not hesitate to say so. He complained to fellow officers that he felt his Tennessee command comprised "too few soldiers to be responsible for so much territory."

Papers and journals told the story of the war to their readers, extolling the virtues of the South, and like *The Index*, hopefully espousing the mutual interests, political and commercial, of Great Britain and the Confederacy.

Preceded by four office-holders of varying degrees of efficiency, James Alexander Seddon became Secretary of War in November of 1862, and was to hold the position almost to the end of hostilities. Biographical sketches of Seddon usually contained the phrase "as a youth, he gave evidence of great promise." But to achieve success in the cabinet, Seddon first had several severe obstacles to overcome in addition to his own frail health which sometimes balked at the long hours he had to work. For one, President Davis was a man who had firm faith in his own insight into military matters and usually did not take gracefully to suggestions from anyone, especially civilian officers. Seddon also dealt with strong-minded generals with strong opinions who, however well they might disguise it, had some degree of contempt for the "meddlesome politicians" back in the Government. Seddon became adept at presenting his own suggestions for the future conduct of the war in such a way as to offend neither the President, who must approve them, nor the generals, who would have to carry them out.

Opposite, instructions for heavy artillery, and drill figures from a manual of arms for volunteers and militia of the Confederate States prepared and issued by the Virginia Military Institute.

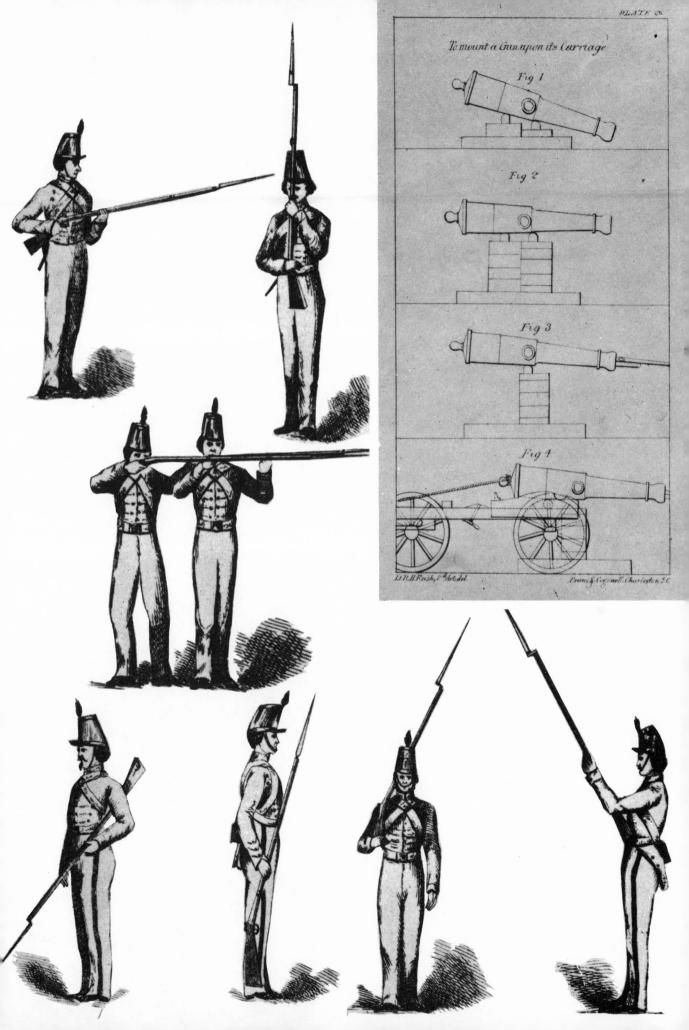

PLATE 25

To mount a Gun upon its Carriage

Fig 1

Fig 2

Fig 3

Fig 4

Sumter appeared in the news again. This published picture of the island redoubt (below) and its accompanying article revealed to Southern readers some improvements made to both the interior and exterior of the building to make it nigh impregnable, so the editors of the publication stated, though they added: "We do not deem it advisable to speak in detail."

Harbors, the cities they served and the seas they opened onto were often in the news. Opposite at top, the rebel steamer *Florida*—formerly the *Oreto*—outruns the U. S. steamship *Oneida* in foreground at the blockade of Mobile. Above is Conrad W. Chapman's oil of two gunboats in Charleston Harbor.

Conscription was looked upon with little favor by some veteran soldiers and officers of both sides. In the less populous South, where many argued that the draft was a Constitutional violation, the quest for new manpower was scraping the bottom of the barrel. The average conscript was a far cry from the splendid volunteer of earlier days. Some of the newcomers were described as of "poor physique, slovenly and insubordinate," and in camps where they made up a goodly proportion, commanding officers reported that: "the dangers of too much applejack and card-playing were painfully evident." In some quarters it was felt that the influx of many such conscripts into the ranks would be dangerous for army morale. Indeed, their induction might well have been disastrous if the character of the army had not already been formed.

Generalizations are unreliable, doubly so concerning men at war. But in the main, it seemed obvious that the conscripts were less enthusiastic about their enforced service than the volunteers who looked upon enlistment as a privilege and an honor. And in some Confederate camps, the number of such men who would take unofficial leave became quite startling. So much so that it was considered expedient to advertise widely the disgrace and punishment awaiting a deserter. He was pictured as an unworthy who would never know the plaudits of his own kin when he came marching home at war's end. And of course, if the worst should happen, he could never know a hero's grave but instead would lie untended where his sins had caught up with him, like some miserable animal, prey for any carrion bird. It is not known whether or not such depictions as the illustration opposite showing "The Fate of a Deserter" had any appreciable effect on those who had made up their minds to take an unscheduled furlough.

John Cabell Breckinridge, Vice-President of the United States, 1857–61, military leader and, later, the last Confederate Secretary of War, is also remembered for his part in the battle of Stone's River. In this action near Murfreesboro, the Confederates drove Rosecrans' army from the field except for one hill crowned with artillery. Breckinridge was ordered to take this strategic high ground. The brunt of the action would fall upon a brigade composed almost entirely of Kentucky soldiers. Breckinridge suspected a trap and thought any attack would be suicidal, but Bragg, under whose orders he acted, was determined to go ahead. It turned out that Breckinridge was right. Soon after the advance started, it was evident that the point to be carried was strongly held by massed Federal artillery. A Union observer described the result thusly: "What a carnival of death followed . . . see the quivering bodies, the stream of blood flowing from a thousand wounds. . . ."

Afterward, Breckinridge, who carried the burden in his heart of having anticipated the dreadful slaughter and then seeing it happen, rode among the decimated ranks of Kentuckians. As he viewed the dead and dying, he was heard to cry out, "Oh my poor Orphans, my poor Orphans," and so the name Kentucky Orphan Brigade became attached to the valiant little band that fought so bravely and so uselessly at Swain's Hill.

Military brains of the Confederacy, Jackson, Joseph Johnston, and
Lee. The South was justifiably proud of its military leaders. Could the
North match them? People below the Mason-Dixon line doubted that.
Federal commanders—and there might be some of passing good ability,
they admitted—fought because it was their job to fight. The Confederate
army leaders were serving a cause.

A Confederate encampment above contrasts with the headquarters of the Army of the Potomac at Brandy Station, Virginia, scene of a memorable cavalry battle between Stuart and Pleasonton where the fighting was most vicious; man-to-man, horse-to-horse until the Federals were finally driven back.

For long, the Southern soldier, when a raid or forward advance caused him to gain and investigate an enemy camp, had compared himself unfavorably with his Yankee opponent in the materials of war and in the foodstuffs so necessary to any fighting man. In charge of Commissary for the South was General Lucius Northrop, a man whose competence was sometimes the butt of jokes even by his friends. The Commissary General's department was encumbered by masses of red tape. The simplest order for rations or forage needed by shifting troops met with all kinds of perplexing delay. In some quarters it was whispered that Northrop stayed on only because he and Davis had been good friends since their days at West Point together. This reason hardly consoled the soldiers in the field who suffered from incompetence in a department as necessary to their welfare as ordnance.

The Battle of Chancellorsville was most memorable for a reason beyond the ebb and flow of struggling armies across a devastated countryside. Though the South again failed to mount a strong offensive even as Union forces drew back, the battle was a Confederate triumph. But at a great price. For Stonewall Jackson gave his life in the victory which Lee wrote to him was "due to your skill and energy." The indomitable Stonewall was shot accidentally by his own men—though some reports claim he was wounded by the enemy—when he returned to his lines from an enthusiastic personal reconnaissance of the retreating foe. His left arm was badly splintered and was amputated soon after.

Stonewall Jackson was an intensely religious man. Once when arms were not forthcoming from Ordnance, Jackson suggested that greater trust was needed in God, whereupon an irreligious soldier proclaimed that there were more prayers in Jackson's camp than muskets. When Lee congratulated him on the course of events at Chancellorsville, Jackson replied, "The General is very kind, but the praise belongs to God."

There were those who remembered him as a stern disciplinarian, a driving drill master. But all respected him as a military leader and as a man. Wearing a battered old flat-topped forage hat that everybody knew, he would bring new heart to those who, upon seeing him, would shout to their fellows over the din of battle, "Here comes Old Jack!"

When Jackson fell wounded from his horse onto the newly won ground near Chancellorsville, aides, rushing to his assistance, scarcely dared guess how serious the injuries were.

critical, in consequence of the violence of
the pneumonia which has attacked him since
he was wounded. Fervent were the prayers
which went up in his behalf from all the
church congregations of the city, yesterday.

P. S.—At a late hour yesterday evening, the
distressing intelligence reached the city, that
Gen. Jackson was dead! He breathed his
last at 3¼ o'clock yesterday afternoon. No
words of ours can express the profound grief
which this sad fact will carry to the hearts of
our people. The language of eulogy now
. . . ration which the name
Jackson inspire, and that . . .
to his loss that requires a . . .
for its indulgence! God will . . .
man to take his place, and will . . .
cause to fail, for want of a cha . . .
is meet and proper that the Co . . . racy, in
all its borders, should grieve this day, for a
GREAT AND GOOD MAN hath fallen.

Gov. LETCHER received the following dispatch last night, by which it will be seen
that the remains of the lamented Jackson
will arrive in this city this afternoon:

To Gov. Letcher—

FREDERICKSBURG, May 10.—Gen. Jackson
died at fifteen minutes past 3 o'clock this
afternoon. His remains will go to Richmond
to-morrow.   A. H. PENDLETON,
                            Major and A. A. G.

We have to thank the public for a favor
shown to our paper beyond our most san-
guine calculations. Our subscription list,
without an effort on our part, and entirely . . .

Vallandigham has been arrested, and was
his trial before a secret court. Considera . . .
excitement sprung up on his arrest, wh . . .
was at Dayton, Ohio, where he resides. . . .
public meeting was called, but was disper . . .
by the military. Two counties, we believe,
under martial law. Vallandigham has
fused to respond to the charges on which
is arraigned. The New York *World* lou . . .
denounces the secrecy with which the p . . .
ceedings . . . . cted, and . . .
. . . . berties wh . . .
. . . . if the pe . . .
. . . . erties! T . . .
. . . . hem ee . . .
. . . . ve y l

THE SENTINEL.
RICHMOND, MONDAY . . . . MAY 11, 1863.

. . . from Europe is interesting.
. . . ritish Parliament was in an uproar over
. . . action of United States Minister Adams
. . . granting a permit or safe-conduct to a ve . . .
. . . trading to Matamoras, because the said
. . . sel was laden with munitions of war for
. . . Mexicans, in their struggle with the Fre . . .
[All other English vessels, trading to . . .
. . . port, have been subjected to an anno . . .
. . . surveillance and search by U. S. cruis . . .
lest supplies might in that way reach . . .
Confederacy.]

Lord Roebuck made a war speech on . . .
occasion; Lord Palmerston was very fir . . .
denouncing Mr. Adams's proceeding; w . . .
Lord Russell was apologetic. [Mr. Sew . . .
will, of course, after a long preliminary . . .
. . . sertation, make things all smooth again . . .
. . . a "cheerful" apology and reparation . . .
. . . quire of foolscap will probably settle . . .
matter. We are not so sure that Fr . . .

None who had served with him could doubt what Jackson's loss would mean to the South. The mortally wounded commander was taken twenty-five miles in an ambulance to the house above, near Guinea's Station. As the days passed, he grew steadily weaker despite every attention from the best available surgeons. Stonewall Jackson's last words were, "Let us pass over the river and rest under the shade of the trees." It was early May of 1863, and now two of the greatest commanders of the South had died. Next day the *Richmond Sentinel* bordered its columns in mourning as the Confederate nation grieved.

--∘◄{ CHAPTER SEVEN }►∘--

JUST AS THE Confederate Government eyed England and France expectantly, those powers watched the progress of the war in America. A conviction in Southern circulation was, "England is still waiting on decisive Confederate victories." Cotton was King in the South. It was pictured on the face of some currency, its name was put on treasury coupons, and it provided the basis for the entire economy. Cotton was the Confederacy's bargaining trump (the South did not know England was overstocked at war's start). Would a cotton embargo against Great Britain change that country's determination to wait-and-watch before taking definite sides? Mr. Benjamin and his department would see. With Mason and Slidell working for him abroad, the hope was always alive that recognition would be forthcoming from these foreign powers.

England needed subtle hints that the Confederates were in earnest and that the two divided and warring territories in North America would never be reunited again. And England needed to be reminded of her own great dependence on cotton. Yet all the South got were the rights of belligerents. Accordingly, John Bull was characterized in the *Southern Illustrated News* as a calculating and greedy personage who preferred to stand on the sidelines, content that whoever won the fight, North or South, he would gain. The North, fearful that the status quo might change and the Confederate States be granted the full recognition they so much desired, pictured the situation differently: Mason and Slidell dicker with Louis Napoleon and John Bull for arms and supplies while the United States, a policeman lurking behind the door, gets ready to wield a nightstick.

THEATRE
OTHELLO.
JOHN BULL
AS
IAGO

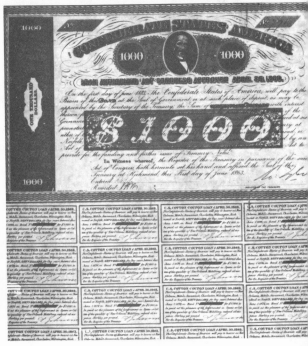

If it seemed to some that the governments and the politicians at home did too little worrying about the soldiers and too much about campaigns, military and political, the soldiers were hardly concerned about the problems of diplomacy and government. Sunday in a Confederate camp, as depicted at left in a famous Sheppard water color, was

given over to other things than worry over Mr. Benjamin's problems. Confederates, and Unionists as well, took what time they could to refurbish their own equipment, to clean and inspect rifles, to reshoe horses and to repair the supply wagons. If there were thoughts of "back home," they were certainly of a more intimate and general nature than wondering how the campaign to enlist Louis Napoleon on the South's side was going. Many of the men had never heard of Mason and Slidell. In the larger troop concentrations where paper and a form of "printing"—usually by pen and pencil—were available, a camp newspaper was issued. There were also some regularly printed joke books for the amusement of the mess. The jokes, needless to say, were often at the expense of the Yankees who were not so much hated throughout the rank and file of Southern soldierdom as they were sympathized with for not knowing any better.

Always though, there was the knowledge that another battle was ahead in some near tomorrow. Veterans who had seen the ranks of their friends thinned played grim betting games among themselves about "who would be wounded next."

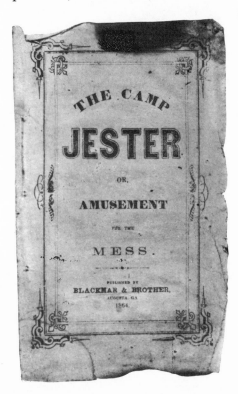

A Confederate soldier handsomely poses before the relatively new-fangled camera against make-believe pastoral scenery. Opposite, an equally peaceful engraving depicts a Union volunteer. In reality, there was little peace for any contestant in a war where there always seemed

to be another battle ahead for those lucky enough to have come through the last one unscathed. After Chancellorsville, initiative lay with the South. And the South chose an invasion of Pennsylvania, ushering in those fated days that culminated in Gettysburg.

Was this a moment of destiny wherein the whole course of the War Between the States might shift against the North? At the Richmond capital, they thought so. Slidell had been encouraged in France. Confederate cotton bonds had been underwritten by a French banking house, and there were more tales that Great Britain was "watching." Needed now was a great military achievement. The necessity to do something came first, and from it evolved the plan to advance directly into enemy country from northernmost Virginia and Shenandoah, into Maryland and Pennsylvania, branching out as opportunity might allow. The plan was audacious and broad. But most of the crucial battle took place in the relatively small area around Gettysburg. The vital breastworks shown below were at Round Top, held by Federal forces whose strong interior lines ran north and then east along ridges and heights culminating in Culp's Hill. To fully encompass the centrally massed troops of the enemy, Longstreet and Lee had to stretch their lines some five miles in a giant elliptical curve.

This was headquarters for George Meade at Gettysburg. The Union general, who had just taken over Hooker's command, deployed his forces along the line of heights that commanded much of the surrounding countryside. The two Round Tops, Big and Little, dominated the battlefield, and from the signal station and lookout posts atop the wooded hills, every Confederate move could be detected and assessed.

General George Pickett, best known for the famous and ill-fated
charge at Gettysburg that bears his name. A fine soldier sent with his
men on a deadly and nigh-impossible mission about which he had written
his fiancée: "My brave Virginians are to attack in front. God in mercy
help us. . . ."

Pickett's task was to take Cemetery Hill, a well-buttressed height strongly held with artillery and commanding a wide open space over which the Confederates had to march before reaching the incline. The area to be traversed was raked by crossfires of shell and shrapnel poured down from the Ridge. Pickett's forces, supported by a Confederate artillery now running perilously low on ammunition due to the thunderous cannonade that preceded the charge, advanced in splendid order with bright banners flying, into the heart of a smoking hurricane of canister, grape and shot.

One of the charges on Cemetery Hill. A charge born of necessity.
A desperate gamble played to the hilt by those supremely brave men;
repulsed by other brave men. This was followed by a slaughter of his

forces that Pickett was never to forget. The enemy fire from the cemetery itself was most heavy. On the grounds of the burial site, a painted sign warned one and all against the use of firearms. . . .

This farmyard at Culp's Hill (above) was turned into a temporary hospital as the angry men of Gettysburg swept back and forth in their passion of destruction. Here, by the wrecked farmhouse and shacks smashed by errant cannon fire, the wounded of both sides rested, too weary and sapped to care whose uniform lay alongside. Some might strengthen to go forward again in the ranks of gray or blue; others had put their muskets aside for the last time. Gettysburg was divided into great silence and then unbelievable sound. First, men had crouched in the fields or on the heights, behind bushes or behind rocks waiting for the signal to go forward, or waiting for the enemy to spring up from some distant ridge and charge headlong. Next, in an instant, quiet would erupt into storm. Soldiers, horses and cannon would thunder into action. And the screams of men and animals mingled with the vibrating thud of artillery as it shook the earth from whose agony dust and smoke arose in a gray curtain as though to shut the dreadful scene off from the rest of the world.

The War Between the States, starting with makeshift armies, grew until hundreds of thousands faced each other in a vast area between New Mexico and the eastern sea. And in all the mounting energy of the conflict that swept across the hills and woods of Tennessee and Virginia and down the Mississippi, the decision for the North at Gettysburg, coming with the fall of Vicksburg, served to "confirm the inevitable," as one of Lincoln's advisers expressed it. The warning was out to Great Britain and France; now there would be no foreign intervention.

188

The Confederates often were forced to fight where they fought—bayonet to saber, cannon to cannon, flag to flag (as in this Currier and Ives print)—because of some factor of supply. The South never willingly abandoned the matériel of war with the same recklessness as did the North, knowing how hard it would be to replace. Better that a decisive action be undertaken while ammunition was not deteriorated through age or depleted by days of sniping and small-scale engagements. Beyond everything, at Gettysburg time, was the overbearing necessity of some positive action. A victory was needed for the Southern cause and a victory could not be attained without risking the chance of battle, even in numbers and on terms more favorable to the enemy. But then facing an enemy of greater strength was customary for the Confederate Army. It was fully believed by officers and men that they fought best against odds. As the lieutenant of a Texas regiment put it: "If ten soldiers of ours suddenly found themselves faced with but ten of the enemy—our men would die of surprise!"

General Lee, astride Traveller, the splendid horse that had carried him through every campaign since the Seven Days around Richmond. Lee once joked to an aide that he really thought Traveller "had something of a sense of military tactics." Some said Lee's "tactics" had failed at Gettysburg, and the Southern commander himself insisted on assuming all responsibility for the defeat and heavy losses. Longstreet, surprised at his chief's determination to make offensive war in the enemy's territory, was inclined to attach blame to this decision which was dictated more by the pressing necessity of the times and so authorized by the Richmond government. As for Lee, long afterward in speaking of Gettysburg, he is reported to have remarked that he thought he could have carried the day if Stonewall Jackson had been at his side.

The dead of both sides lay everywhere. More than five thousand of them, in the fields and on the rock-dotted slopes. The wounded were indistinguishable from those beyond help except that perhaps here and there an arm might be thrown up in pain or to ward off the hot rays of the sun. On this open space near Seminary Ridge (above) the Union general, Reynolds, was killed in the early phases of battle, while below, Slaughter Pen earns its name as bodies dot the foot of Round Top.

A rifle appropriately marking his final resting place, this sharp-shooter lies on the ground, his heart found by a bullet from another sharpshooter, his counterpart on the other side. Others lay in shallow trenches, curled up as though to sleep off the dreadful nightmare of battle, like the dead Confederate soldier, below.

A fact of life was the care of the dead. Men could not be left life-less where they had fallen, and there was a sarcastic joke in one Northern paper that "at least the embalmers were making capital out of the war." Burials were so many as to become simple ceremonies with very little adornment. Only the silent sadness of comrades marked most farewells to fellow soldiers entrusted tenderly to the ground.

If the surgeon who repaired the wounded was important, important also was the one who prepared the dead. This was a grisly job, often performed hastily as near the front lines as possible, in a tent or building specially set aside for the process. Soldiers passing by usually averted their eyes, saying to companions that "they would rather charge into battle than walk past that tent."

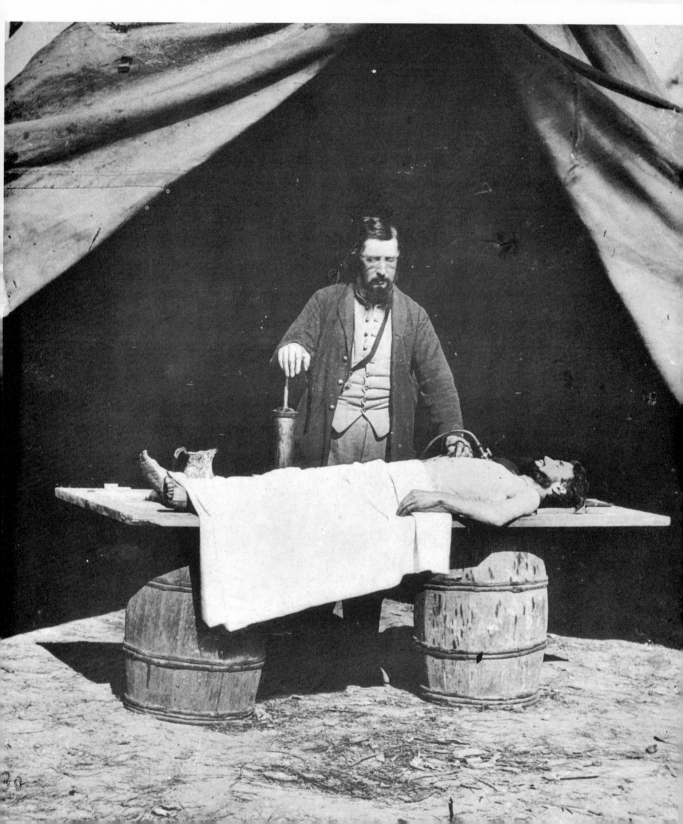

Stragglers coming back from the front, as Sheppard visualized them with his brush and water colors. Defeated or victorious, it was good for an army and its soldiers to come home from enemy country; to come home where faces and people along the way were no longer hostile or aloof but considerate and generous. Meantime, in Richmond and further into the South a pall of depression had spread over the land from the misadventures in Pennsylvania and at stronghold Vicksburg. "Will we ever recover from the fatal trip to Gettysburg?" was a question heard on many sides.

In the Southern cities parties were still merry, but war reached out a long reminder to such home front gaiety as chaperons remarked on the number of cripples attending. It is said that some unmarried girls used to complain good-naturedly and not unkindly among themselves about "the halt, the lame and the ailing" from whose numbers they would have to choose their future husbands. Still, the romantic instincts of young people were not seriously affected, and the apt phrase "Cupid on crutches" was thought quite amusing by the girls as well as by the "Cupids" themselves.

-·◦◄{ CHAPTER EIGHT }►◦·-

A ROUND THE FOURTH OF JULY, 1863, just as the dreadful news of
Gettysburg had come to a South praying for a great victory,
there was further word of misfortune to Confederate arms.
Vicksburg, the strongest bastion and key defense of the southeastern
area, surrendered. For eight months Grant had schemed to open up the
Mississippi River. But the guns of Vicksburg at a strategic bend of the
stream blocked the waterway effectively. If Vicksburg could be taken,
the whole river would fall into Federal hands. Farragut's fleet, after the
capture of New Orleans, had steamed up the river past Vicksburg the
summer before without being more than annoyed by the shore batteries.
But, as Farragut advised the military chiefs, he and Porter and their
sailors could not take land fortifications. Substantial land forces were
necessary. And Grant, in charge of the area for the Union, felt unsafe
as long as the Confederates held Vicksburg. Under the over-all command
of Joseph Johnston, John Pemberton, a Pennsylvanian who had served
in Mexico with Grant, had to please both the commands of Johnston
and also the whims of Davis who had strong ideas on how the Mississippi
campaign should be run. Sometimes commands conflicted, and poor
Pemberton would be caught in the middle.

The ground around Vicksburg was favorable to defense. The
precipitous bluffs containing fortifications overlooked the river, whose
whole width at this sudden bend in the stream could be swept by Confederate cannon. The land both toward the Yazoo upriver and in the
opposite direction was poor, containing many bogs and areas of quick-
sand. Directly behind, as above, the Confederates were also well forti-

fied. "Whistling Dick," also shown above, was a famous cannon of this campaign. Union soldiers called the gun by name and swore the whistle of the projectile was unmistakable. The U. S. Navy held the river; Johnston's forces had been cut off from Pemberton's. Rations inside Vicksburg were short, and the fortress city took an unmerciful pounding from numbers of 11- and 13-inch mortars across the river as well as a tightening ring of Union artillery elsewhere. Plainly the siege could have but one end, and on July 3, 1863, Pemberton met with Grant to arrange terms. The formal surrender of Vicksburg was consummated the next day.

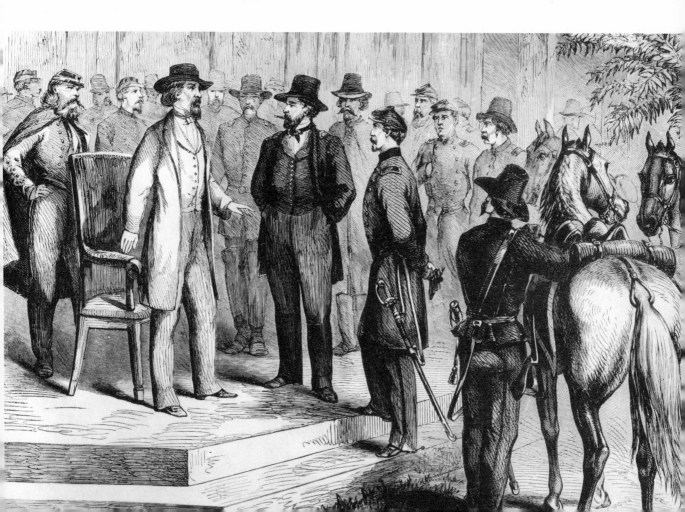

While the Confederacy was suffering from a multiplicity of ailments that ran from military defeats on the battlefield and dissensions in the government to disappointments in foreign relations and shortages in all things, the North too had its troubles. The first passions and enthusiasms had waned; war weariness and disgust grew as the conflict became a prolonged, fratricidal struggle. In the summer of 1863 there was particular discontent just when the Union should have been enthused by victories in the field.

Many people were saying loudly that the war was a failure and should be discontinued. Conscription, making war service no longer voluntary but coercive, was unpopular. Officials in Washington were aware that there were organized conspiracies to defeat the draft. In July, riots against conscription started in New York. Police were unable to control the surging mobs, and as militia tried unsuccessfully to disperse the crowds by firing over their heads, casualties mounted. The protest against conscription later resulted in indiscriminate violence and looting. There were many deaths, including several Negroes who were hung and burned. To many in the crowd, the innocent Negro was a symbol of all the trouble. Order was not restored until soldiers of the Seventh Regiment marched into the city late one night, clumping up cobble-stoned streets that seemed to empty magically at their approach.

Here were important men, three surgeons posed with a "body servant" taken at the hospital in Lynchburg, Virginia. The entire medical corps of the South numbered less than three thousand, and it had been said that each doctor was as valuable as five hundred soldiers. Many of the physicians performed their tasks near the field of action. Amputations were commonplace, and mortality ran high due to the high incidence of gangrene. Illness was an even greater problem than war wounds. Measles in the early period, typhoid fever, malaria and dysentery were the chief offenders among men in the service. In the treatment of wounds and illnesses, the doctors were faced with a constant shortage of medicines. For lack of the real thing—such as morphine and opium, quinine and calomel—the Confederate medical man turned to substitutes. Surgical instruments and equipment were also in short supply, and ordinary knives sometimes had to serve as scalpels.

Smuggling much-needed medicines into the South was an activity of importance sufficient to attract the efforts of patriotic citizens and soldiers alike. It also attracted the attention of Adalbert Volck, who engraved this scene of vital medical supplies being brought into the Confederate States by some circuitous route. Bandages were somewhat less of a problem than biologicals and drugs, for the women scraped sheets and clothes for lint; rags were the nearest things available for sponges, while horsehair was made to do for sutures. The heroics of the battlefield soldiers, the glamour and beauty of the belles who entertained those heroes has been plentifully painted in words and picture. But no appraisal of the wartime South is complete without due acknowledgment to the doctors and their equally gallant women aides who labored cease-lessly against incredible obstacles to cure the wounded and sick and ease the agony of the incurable.

By now President Davis was calling upon the citizens of the Confederacy to plant food rather than tobacco and cotton. A belated and not too successful effort was made to standardize the various gauges and operational systems of the Southern railroads. The problem of sustaining life on home front and battlefront was paramount. And the sacrifices made for the soldiers were well worth it. Many a family scrimped outrageously and "shopped" around when certain articles were not easily buyable, to equip a beloved soldier for the field.

Women not otherwise occupied were constantly sewing or knitting, making things, mending what they had. The price of material skyrocketed; though blockade runners and the underground from Baltimore brought in bolts of pretty drygoods, the *Richmond Enquirer* commented wryly that "Even those who can afford the very high prices of the profiteers can't!" Latest styles were still shown in papers. But the accompanying articles were always careful to describe to a land where silks were a thing of the past how the Southern woman could make her own "new fashions" out of North Carolina homespun.

War bred rumors. And those rumors unencumbered by facts seemed to spread fastest. Perhaps a man "who knew an officer who had a friend who had been in command of this Confederate gun at Morris Island" might have heard the one that Davis and Lincoln were in some dark conspiracy to prolong the war to perpetuate their own authority. There were other stories that the Yankees were trying to spread disease among the animals of the Confederate cavalry. This caused some genuine fearfulness to a side whose horse supply seemed in a steadily declining state of numbers and health. Then, one of the officers in Beauregard's command sketched what he believed was a most deadly missile: "a poisoned ball, fired from a small rifled cannon by the Yankees showing our countrymen and the world at large what foul engines of war the dastardly and discomfitted foe are using against us."

Sumter in the news again. This time, though, the attacking shoe
was on the other foot. Union forces were now bombarding the Confederates, and defenders in gray scattered when heavy shells from the
big Parrott guns on Morris Island exploded around the island fort.
Sumter was badly battered but not taken. This was July of 1863, a black
month for Confederate arms and hopes.

Conversation subjects in army camps were as varied as the rumors. There was the excitement of exchanging information and tall tales with men from other battle theatres, and it was said that if a good soldier knew nothing, he made something up. The art of "patchwork" on ragged uniforms became quite an occupation, and there were heated arguments as to who had the best sewing technique. Over victuals someone would put forth the opinion that Lee would have won at Gettysburg if Stuart had come up. Someone else would tell fabulous tales of Morgan's ride to Indiana and Ohio. Much of the time there was a yearning to go home that soldiers of all times have known, yet found hard to express even to those they knew felt the same way. In the scene at left, one homesick warrior with a sense of humor has put up a sign advertising the "Spotswood Hotel," the plush hostelry of notables in Richmond.

Harper's Weekly shows Longstreet's sharpshooters firing on a Federal supply train, left. This was an appendage of Chickamauga, and the attempt of General Rosecrans to push Bragg out of Chattanooga. Bragg left Chattanooga without a fight, only to gather to him the extra strength of Longstreet, enough to whip Rosecrans at Chickamauga and drive him back upon Chattanooga; as a Northern paper put it, "a fine ending to what had started as a triumphal march through western Tennessee."

"We have fought the Battle of Chickamauga to gain our position at Chattanooga, and here we are!" ridiculed the *Southern Illustrated News* apropos of Rosecrans' hopeful advance and subsequent retreat.

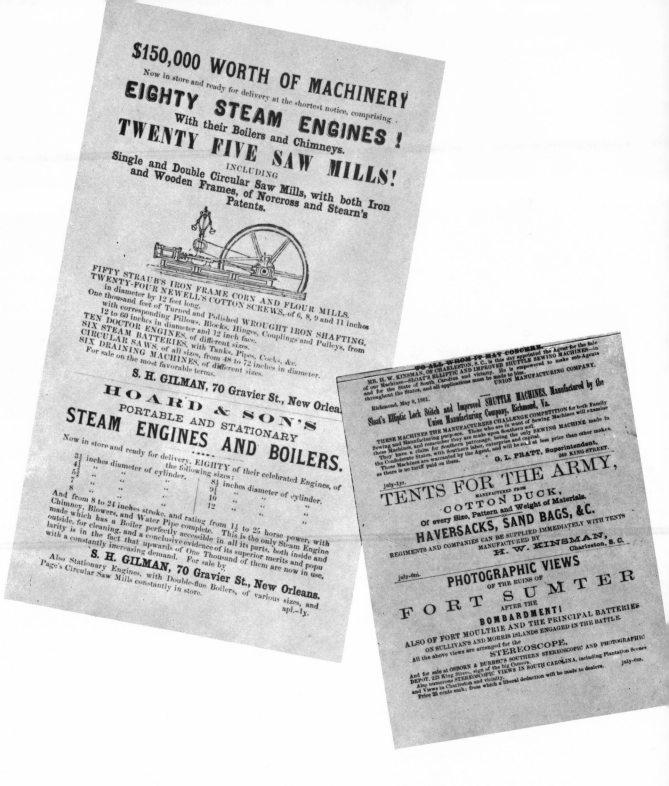

These were signs of the times; from sewing machines "made upon Southern soil" to tents for the army and "photographic views of Fort Sumter after the bombardment." These ads from *De Bow's Review* in the early part of the war changed in character as the months passed. New Orleans advertised steam engines and boilers, but at one time a Southern buyer, after making inquiries, sorrowfully reported that "all they had left were the sketches."

NOTICE.

To the Farmers of Campbell, Franklin, Henry, Patrick, Grayson, Carroll, Floyd, the Western part of Pittsylvania and Halifax, and the Southern part of Bedford Counties :

The surplus Forage in the above district has been set apart for the purpose of feeding the Public Animals not in service.

All the Corn, Rye, Oats, Hay, Fodder and Straw, not required for the use of the people in the above Counties and parts of Counties, will be wanted by the Government for the purpose above stated.

Stables are being erected at suitable stations in the District, at which Farmers will be expected to deliver their surplus Forage, and for which they will be paid the prices fixed by the State Commissioners. The following are the Schedule Prices at present :

Corn unshelled, $3,95 per bushel; Corn shelled, $4,00 per bushel; Rye, $3,20 per bushel; Oats, $2,00 per bushel; Sheaf Oats, $3,70 per 100 lbs.; Hay, per 100 lbs. $3,00; Wheat Straw, $1,30 per 100 lbs; for baling Long Forage, 50 cts. per 100 lbs.; for hauling Long Forage, 8 cents per mile per 100 lbs.; for hauling Corn, 4 cents per bushel per mile.

It is with great difficulty that the necessary transportation for armies in the field can be furnished. The Government, therefore, cannot supply the teams to haul the Forage from the farms to the stations at which it is needed. It will be necessary for the farmers to do the transportation, for which, they will be paid liberal prices.

JAS. G. PAXTON,
Maj. and Q. M.

Fair Grounds, near Lynchburg, Nov. 13th, 1863.

JOHNSON & SCHAFFTER PRINTERS. LYNCHBURG, VA.

In a land that desperately needed to make the most of what little it had, problems of supply were complicated by more than natural limitations. It was true that the South was short on manufacture and machine tools, on transportation, on matériel of nearly every description. But at the same time, there was the paradox of plenty in the midst of want. Some farmers were accused of withholding ample foodstocks from the market or else charging all the traffic would bear. Meanwhile, officers complained that there was not enough forage for the animals of cavalry and supply trains. And it was darkly suspected that some commands were more fortunate in this respect than others. The Confederate Congress was certainly not rising in the public's estimation, while throughout the land citizens could tell tales of graft, speculation and favoritism of all kinds, which sometimes seemed more dangerous to the South's cause than all the Yankee armies put together.

213

Those who might get rich from the war by profiting from shortage and those who looked the other way in the government seemed little concerned with the state of semi-starvation which affected a good proportion of the population. People with money, enough money, could still get what they wanted. People without means could, as one speculator brazenly put it, "Grow fat on their starvation." The bread riot in Richmond in 1863 was a spontaneous overflow of such inequities and and the long-standing grievances stemming from them. The trouble started when a group of women collected outside a government building to protest. Such hunger demonstrations were not unique. But this time the crowd and the excitement grew apace until suddenly the mob surged off through the streets of the city, forcing their way into bakeries and food stores as they went, brushing aside proprietors and loading their arms with goods. Though some officials claimed the rioting had been instigated by "rowdies," the action of these hungry women certainly was not extraordinary when they themselves could see the advertisements—as above—of Charleston candy manufacturers, their fancy confectioneries and equally fancy prices, catering to the more fortunate.

There were other shortages. For instance, engravers were needed desperately in the South. Not alone to make the bills of currency and official documents, but also, as here, to help in journalistic enterprises for the public entertainment.

In a conflict between huge masses of mèn on the scale of the War Between the States, the number of prisoners taken by both sides was enormous. With food so precious in overcrowded Richmond—which was now a prison center—there were those who loudly suggested that one way to save food was not to feed the prisoners so well. At Libby Prison (above) captive Union officers complained of hunger and over-crowding, but few of them realized their fare was as good as that of many a Southerner at home or in the field. Belle Isle (below) in the James River, formerly a picnic spot for Richmonders, was thought worse than Libby. Shelter of any kind was rare, the same scarcity of tents familiar to the Southern armies meant that Union prisoners often had to sleep outside in all kinds of weather.

Both Libby and Belle Isle prisons quickly earned bad reputations in the North. On some fronts U. S. officers warned: "It's better to get shot than captured by Johnny Reb." The South had its own version, comparing the "solitary confinement of a Confederate prisoner in an Ohio penitentiary" at right with the "fine treatment" accorded Federal prisoners on Belle Isle, below. Later, as the war went on, when captives were shifted to places in the deeper South like Andersonville, Georgia, conditions worsened and bitterness on both sides grew. Publicly, each side stoutly maintained that all sin and malpractice was the exclusive property of the other. Yet there were many attempts by officials on both sides to make the prison "sentence" more humane, as illustrated by the document shown.

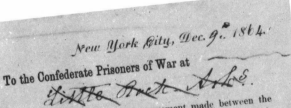

New York City, Dec. 9ᵗʰ 1864.

To the Confederate Prisoners of War at
~~little Rock Ark E.~~

Under the late arrangement made between the Confederate States and the United States, to each supply their own Prisoners of War with necessary supplies, I have been selected to carry out, on part of the Confederate States, this arrangement. I therefore desire that you will, AT ONCE, determine, by a committee or otherwise, the supplies (Clothing, Blankets, and Provisions,) you most need: give the number of blankets and each article of clothing, naming those articles first that you need most. 2d. Give the number of officers, privates, and citizens separate. 3d. Select ~~double~~ officers give their NAME, RANK, AND REGIMENT IN FULL, who you desire to receive and issue to you the supplies on their arrival.

I am, very respectfully,
    Your Obedient Servant,
        Wᵐ N. R. Beall

BRIG.-GEN., P. A. C. S.,
Confederate Agent to supply Prisoners of War.

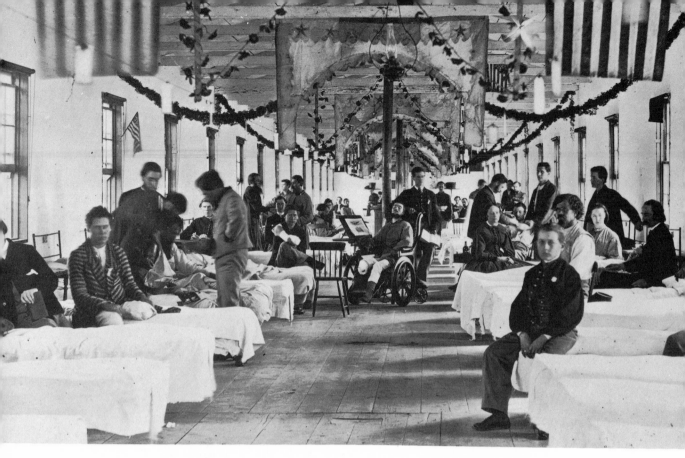

A banner-bedecked, bright-looking hospital such as this Northern one for military personnel was virtually unknown below the Mason-Dixon line. Even though some Union prisoners came back with happy tales of how they had been allowed to play baseball (below) in an encampment in North Carolina, papers in the North occasionally com-

MEDICAL COLLEGE HOSPITAL.

The FACULTY regret to be under the necessity of announcing a further advance in the charges of this establishment. Experience has proved that at the present exorbitant prices of provisions, medicines, &c., it is impossible to keep the hospital in operation on its present receipts. The Legislature has just passed a bill allowing to the jailor for the maintenance of prisoners, $2 50 per diem; and for some time past, the charge for board in the private jails of this city has been $3 per day. At present prices, these rates cannot be considered excessive. The patrons of the hospital, therefore, cannot expect that it shall continue to receive patients—furnishing not only board, but medical attendance and costly medicines—at the present charges, which, for the great bulk of the patients, are lower than the above mentioned charges for board alone.

On and after the 15th of October, the charges will be as follows, both for patients then remaining in the hospital, and for those admitted from that time:

White persons in private rooms, . . . $5 per day.
    "   "   public ward, . . . 4 "
Negroes, ... 3 "

As heretofore, a small fee will be charged for Surgical Operations, and a fee of $10 for cases of Midwifery.

In cases of *Mania a Potu*, the charge will be $8 per day, invariably in advance.

L. S. JOYNES, M. D.,
President.

Richmond, Oct. 7, 1863.

plained in print that those of their captured, if wounded, "are not given proper care by the Rebels." But it was increasingly expensive to be sick or hurt, even for a Southerner in his own land. The hospitals were crowded. There was too much illness to be cured and never, it seemed, enough nursing hands or medicines. Like food or clothing, or anything else a citizen of the Confederate States cared to look at, hospital rates, likewise, had to rise.

While people at home complained and journals published such cartoons as this one of a fat mouse labeled "Chairman of Committee on 'Subsistence,'" the men with General Longstreet's command were in the process of attacking Knoxville.

When Bragg was driven from the heights about Chattanooga, Longstreet was forced to withdraw into northeastern Tennessee. The retreat from Knoxville was notable for the terrible weather that prevailed; supply wagons, and soldiers, many of them with no boots or shoes, wallowed in the mud. One of Longstreet's men wrote some words about the shoeless condition of the army. It inspired the publication of a drawing entitled "An Appeal to the Mothers and Daughters of the South," which appeared in *Southern Punch*, opposite, and eventually a good supply of shoes was sent to Longstreet.

James Longstreet, a squarely built man of tenacious opinion and spirit, a veteran of many campaigns, was one of the few who ever publicly (or privately, probably) questioned the strategy of that supreme

commander of them all, Robert E. Lee. Longstreet (above) had great confidence in his own military judgments; most likely this was what led to his "second-guessing" of Lee on Gettysburg. General Longstreet considered himself a more capable leader when he felt he was essentially on his own, not required to reconcile his opinion or argue out his strategems with other commanders.

CONFEDERATE DAVID.

Torpedo Boat   40 to 60ft long x 5 to 7ft Diam. Built of wood or iron.

Built 1863

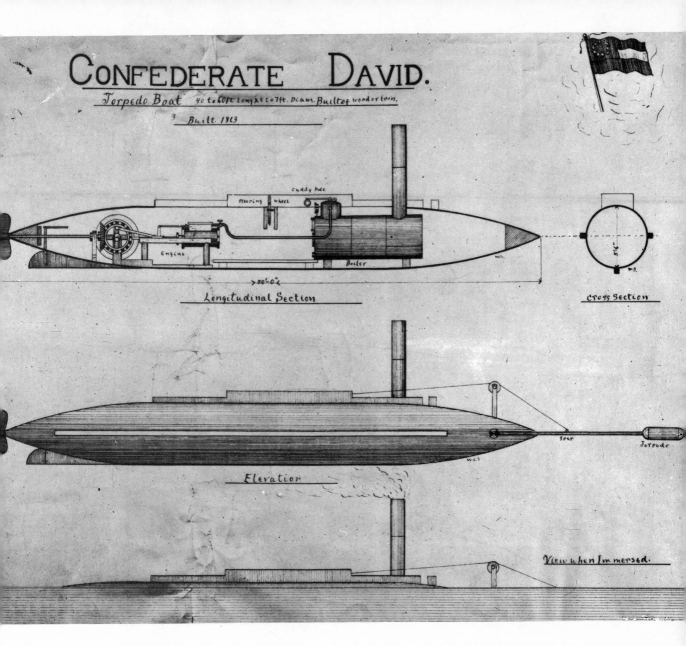

Longitudinal Section

Cross Section

Elevation

View when Immersed.

While men at Fort Moultrie and with Battery Bee on Sullivan's Island stood guard, other defenders of Charleston were planning ways of retaliating by water against the large fleet of Union warships that stood off the harbor. Confederate defense ideas and machines of war were often unorthodox. If scarcities necessitated the makeshift, they also stimulated the imagination. Blueprints are shown of the torpedo ship *David* with which the defenders hoped to make up for their inferiority in many conventional ways. The *David* may be considered one of the first torpedo boats; its explosive charge was attached to a long spar fitted into the prow. But Confederate naval authorities placed so little faith in what one of them called an "absurd" vessel that the *David* had to be built on funds from private citizens.

People who saw Jefferson Davis on Richmond streets thought the President looked tired and worried. One worry held by many concerned how the slave population might react to the various blandishments of Northern propaganda. Union firebrands expected "a general uprising of slaves against their oppressors." Their disappointment when this did not happen was as marked as Southern satisfaction. At home a cartoon poked fun at a usually well fed slave who'd gone to live with the Yankees, then had to be "nursed back to health," and people recalled that a Union soldier making remarks to another slave got called "a nasty abolition Yankee" in reply. But when labor was needed for fortifications, slaves could be, and were, impressed into service.

Ulysses S. Grant, was now Supreme Commander of all Federal forces, the first time Congress had bestowed this rank on a military leader since 1779. By now Confederate fighting strength was mainly concentrated in Lee's Army of Northern Virginia and Johnston's Army of Tennessee. The Battle of the Wilderness in May of 1864 was heralded by some Union soldiers in their letters home as one which might very well finish Lee. It was no secret to the Federals that those on the other side were down to rations hardly suitable for fighting men— crackers and a little fat meat supplemented by ground corncobs, husks and sawdust.

It was a heavily armed, well-fed and comparatively rested army of Grant's that surged into battle against the tired, ragged legions in homespun in the dreary, dank land of the Wilderness. Even in daylight the wooded areas were gloomy; maneuver was most difficult, and scouts came to rely much more on their ears than their eyes.

Spotsylvania, of the Wilderness campaign, introduced trench warfare to the science of war strategy. Grant's losses were roughly three times more than Lee's, but as the Federal ranks were thinned by the well-entrenched Confederates, there always seemed to be endless reserves to spring into line. Lee had no such resources and, indeed, was to lose one of his most priceless assets. For in the act of leading his cavalry around Yellow Tavern to harass Sheridan, the incomparable Jeb Stuart was mortally wounded by a bullet. Although General Stuart averred that while he was willing to die, he hoped to get over it, the wound proved fatal a few hours later. The command of his troops fell to Fitzhugh Lee (above) who was to hold Sheridan from Richmond even as Grant was thwarted in the dismal swamps and bogs of the Wilderness.

There was a mild furor in the North when a paper in New England commented scathingly on the way Grant and other Federal generals were consistently being checkmated by Southern commanders, particularly Robert E. Lee. The conclusion, stated in no uncertain terms, was that Confederate generalship must be far superior to the Union variety. There had been considerable criticism in the North over Lincoln's handling of the army and the rotation of its commanders. Stories of Grant's drinking were suspected of being exaggerated, yet people reasoned there must be a foundation of truth beneath so much rumor. Northerners who had been told often of the "superiority" of their armies and at the same time, how poorly things were going for the "Rebels" who continued to

fight, as a Boston paper put it, only "out of sheer obstinacy," wondered why the fighting dragged on, and many of them came to accept the brilliance of Lee and his fellow-commanders. Above, Confederate works at Cold Harbor, Virginia, while below, collecting remains of the dead on a battlefield where Grant for a time would not call a truce to bury his dead; an action which caused the Confederates to say, "He plans to stink us out!"

By now many officers and men on both Union and Confederate sides knew how the conflict must end. A lieutenant of Sherman's command once rode out of his way by mistake, and the return to Union lines took him through the countryside of the enemy. "Want is written on every face," he reported when he gained his own camp. Federal soldiers told one another that Johnny Reb was fighting on from habit, for "he must know he can no longer win." Certainly Grant's policy of attrition was having an effect. Accused of being callous about his own losses, Grant operated on the mathematically sound principle that two or three casualties in his own forces were fair exchange for one on the Confederate side.

On some sections of the front, pickets on outpost duty actually fraternized with one another. At times the war was monotonous even for the men who fought it and who might be killed in it the very next minute. At such places as Vicksburg, at Knoxville, along the Rapidan, to mention but a few, soldiers actually "visited" across the lines. Officers were usually angry to find out about such fraternizing, feeling that it would not make for the right spirit in the next battle. But the unconventional practice continued occasionally and, in the doing, warriors of both sides discovered that "those fellows over there aren't as bad as we've been told; they're human too."

-·⊰{ CHAPTER NINE }⊱·-

ON THE SEAS, the Confederates did the best they could with what they could build, refit or capture. After nearly two years of high success as a destroyer of commerce the *Alabama*, under the command of one of the foremost Confederate naval heroes of the war, Raphael Semmes, was to meet her doom in the summer of 1864. This most famous of all Confederate raiders was in Cherbourg Harbor for repairs when the U. S. warship *Kearsarge* also entered the French port. Semmes soon extended a challenge to the Union captain that once he could lay in coal, he would be glad to sail the *Alabama* into battle. The *Kearsarge* was superior to her opponent in the size of crew, in fire power and in speed. It was also well protected by chain cables hung over the freeboards. Despite these handicaps, Semmes and the *Alabama* gave as good as they got until the discouraging discovery was made that much of the *Alabama's* powder was defective. A well-directed heavy shell thrown into the stern of the *Kearsarge* failed to explode, and with that miscarriage of gunnery justice, Semmes' last chance of victory was gone. Sometime later, the *Alabama* received her death blow, listed precariously (opposite) and then sank stern first while the heavy guns of the *Kearsarge* (top picture) continued to fire with devastating effect.

Another naval matter concerned Farragut's victory at Mobile Bay, closing one of the last major ports of the South. Farragut's force, led by his own *Hartford*, included a fleet of more than a dozen wooden ships and four ironclad monitors. The Confederates had the shore batteries of Fort Morgan and a string of "homemade" torpedoes laid in the bay. Behind this was the Confederate fleet, pathetic in quantity and quality compared to the Union armada. All the Southerners could muster were three wooden gun barges and the ironclad ram *Tennessee* (above).

Farragut of "Damn the torpedoes" fame quickly got through this first line of defense though several of his ships were damaged. This brought him face to face with the defending fleet of four. The three small gunboats were quickly shelled out of action and the entire Confederate effort fell on the *Tennessee*, commanded by Admiral Franklin Buchanan, hero of the *Virginia's* adventures at Hampton Roads two and a half years earlier. Though every ship in the big Union fleet turned its fire upon him, Buchanan fought the *Tennessee* defiantly. Again and again, the ram charged the whole Union line of ships; at one point the *Tennessee* came so close to Farragut's *Hartford* that the sides of the two vessels touched each other briefly before drifting apart again. By now Admiral Buchanan was seriously wounded but refused to give up the unequal battle and fought gallantly on. Finally, the *Tennessee* lost her funnel. Next, her rudder was rendered useless, and at the same time her engines failed her. Only then was the battle ended.

This was Atlanta, Georgia Though soldiers often marched in the streets, and wounded sometimes lay on depot platforms, the worst of the war had not yet come to Atlanta. Everyone fervently hoped it would not, even as the name "Sherman" was being learned by every tongue.

William Tecumseh Sherman looks over the land he will follow to Atlanta and on across Georgia to the sea. With Grant fully occupying Lee and the Army of Northern Virginia, Sherman's task was to close on Johnston's Army of Tennessee, destroy Southern arms as he went and gain the vital rail hub of Atlanta, if possible. Virtually from the Ohio Valley, Sherman made his line of march down the railroad line that ran to the Southeast—again railroads were to play a vital part in the over-all strategy. "The Atlanta campaign would have been impossible without the railroads," Sherman once said. As his line of communications lengthened with the depth of his penetration into Confederate country, Sherman, facing Johnston's strenuous opposition, grew more worried about his rear. The whereabouts of the Confederate Forrest and his cavalry concerned the Union general whose entire army was dependent for some time on that so-vulnerable lifeline to the rear.

As Sherman came closer, burning and fighting his way along, the Confederate fortifications on the Chattanooga railroad line before Atlanta watched and waited. There were too few men, too few cannon, insufficient ammunition. But the defenders vowed to slay some Yankees. One Union soldier to be killed riding into the Confederate lines was Major General James McPherson (below). At the war's start years earlier, McPherson sagely predicted to a West Point classmate that the war would be no "ninety-day" affair but a long drawn out struggle.

Buildings in and around Atlanta looked like this, before and after. Below on corner is the main bank of the city after the heavy siege-fire from Sherman's artillery preluded his entrance into Atlanta. In Sherman and in Grant, Lincoln had finally found two Union generals who seemed to be tenacious and—as one Washington paper put it—"almost as inspired in leadership and strategy as the Rebel leaders."

Taking what they could, the citizens of Georgia fled from the path of Sherman's army. Those wishful thinkers who had likened the Union general's advance to that of Napoleon at Moscow were sadly disappointed. But, paradoxically, Sherman grew less dependent on supplies brought great distances as he marched further into enemy country. For now he had gained a territory that could supply his every need, and his resourceful soldiers became adept at living off the land.

Of course it was apparent to Sherman that his communications were under constant threat, with Forrest and Hood loose somewhere at his rear. In September of 1864 Atlanta was taken by Sherman. Two months later the Union general (opposite) fired the city: "It is no more use to me; it shall be of no use to the enemy."

Sherman's march to the sea—driving the citizens of Georgia from his path, living off their crops and livestock and land—was virtually unopposed. Here and there groups of angry men, some citizens, some soldiers from brigades which had been all but wiped out, joined together for guerrilla action and did what they could to harass the Federal advance as it swept across the country. Irked by the surrender of Atlanta, some of these bands carried rude flags proclaiming "No more surrenders" and meant what they said. It was some small recompense for those who had had their homes pillaged and set afire by the Yankees to hear from a guerrilla band that they had picked off some Federals from ambush. Meanwhile, Sherman did not forget the railroad, determined that his own avenue of communication and advance was not to aid the Confederates. Where strategy so dictated, his men industriously tore up tracks, destroyed stations, sheds and sidings and fired strings of wooden freight cars, leaving behind only the iron wheels (opposite). Then Sherman turned at Savannah and started north. In places where resistance was expected, such as parts of South Carolina whose Fort Putnam, Charleston, is shown at right, Northern officers conveniently looked the other way and thus soldiers were encouraged in their systematic looting and razing of the countryside.

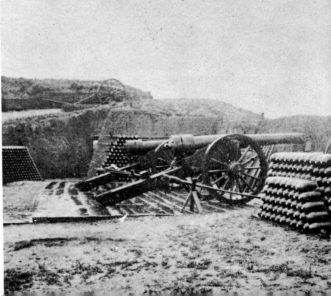

In charge of South Carolina defenses was Hardee, with Wade Hampton, who had taken Stuart's place as chief of cavalry, also on hand. The main Confederate strength was in and around Charleston. Hampton, a brilliant soldier whose intuitive grasp of strategy and tactics often kept him ahead of many of his confreres, suggested that a thrust at one or another segment of Sherman's broadly spread advancing army was advisable as alternative to waiting for the Union general to attack at his pleasure. But Hampton's advice was not taken, and the small garrison at Charleston waited for the inevitable onslaught while shells burst in the streets and the citizenry prepared for evacuation. Some officials swore that if Charleston fell, the Confederate cause would suffer its death blow, but invariably there were those who sounded this same refrain as each of the South's cities was threatened successively.

The railroad station at Charleston looked like this by the time Hardee evacuated the port. Meanwhile Columbia, the capital of South Carolina and in its interior, had already fallen. The city was virtually destroyed by fire which both sides accused the other of having set.

More and more—aside from the main army groups left, principally Lee's and Joe Johnston's—operations took on the haphazard, poorly co-ordinated character of disorganized men fighting in a dismembered land. The railroads, so vital to the South, had been systematically destroyed wherever possible by Union operations. The creaks in the economy had become cracks, and the barter system was more reliable than currency. Men still fought, but many did so now as individuals, or in small groups like these Confederate sharpshooters waiting to fire on the camouflaged Union vessel creeping upstream.

246

Matters were no better in Virginia than in the deeper South. The men, whose half-rations had now become quarter-rations, supplemented their inadequate diet by eating whatever wild growing things they could. One of General Lee's staff is reported to have said: "In addition to the usual disadvantages, we have the unique one of being closest to the Union supply-source of fresh, unlimited manpower." And it seemed more difficult to supply Confederate troops but twenty miles from Richmond than for the Union to supply its forces in Virginia from New York machine shops or Massachusetts factories, a matter of several hundred miles. Railroad rates continued to mount as the efficiency of the still-operating roads declined even further, and there were troubles with the military telegraph, as Beauregard more than once complained.

NOTICE.

RICHMOND, FREDERICKSBURG AND POTOMAC RAILROAD.

By a resolution of the Board of Public Works adopted on the 20th day of July, 1864, the tolls on freights over this Road were authorized to be ten times the rates of toll established by the Board of Directors on the 1st of May, 1861, which rates were by the Board of Directors of this Company adopted on the 27th of July, 1864, except as to tolls on wood, which were then established at eight times the rate fixed by the tariff of May 1, 1861.

☞To take effect August 1, 1864.

This drawing, "made from life" by a special artist of the *Southern Illustrated News*, shows a Confederate soldier on picket duty at Lee's onetime headquarters at Drewry's Bluff. One soldier on leave, seeing such a sketch and then ruefully surveying himself and his tattered raiments, allowed as how he had never seen such a handsomely appointed fellow "around the real war" as was pictured in the sketch.

By now Richmond had seen its traditional Revolutionary cannon—formerly fighting the silent artillery battle such monuments do—confiscated and sent to the Tredegar Iron Works to be melted down for the makings of new cannon. Tredegar and the Atlanta works provided much of the cannon, shot and armor-plating used by the Confederacy. Tredegar, whose smoking chimneys and sprawling buildings lay between the swift-moving James and the narrow Kanawha Canal, stands out particularly as one of the most efficient of Southern manufacturing industries. Soldiers had a certain confidence in the Tredegar war products which was generally justified, though several of the big Parrott guns from there had exploded at Fredericksburg and some of the ammunition failed to detonate properly.

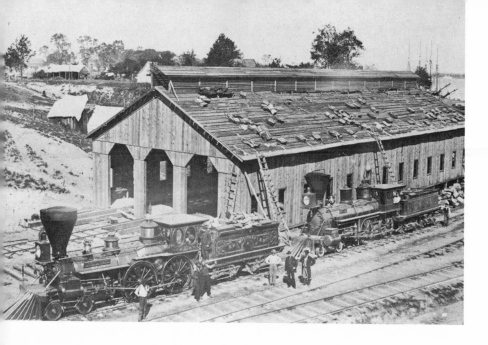

"The busiest place in all the United States" was the description
given to City Point, Virginia (above) whose deep-water port on the
James River welcomed tall-masted supply ships from the North, while a
military railroad could carry the matériel on to Grant's line at Petersburg. The railroad workers around the two locomotives ("finer than any
the Rebels ever saw," they boasted) know their picture is being taken

here, and they stop vital work around the engine house long enough to look up. Here are products of the blast furnaces, the factories and the ordnance plants of the North, funneled through City Point and thus on to Grant. These stocks of Union war supplies seemed to grow more plentiful even as Confederate officers often had their men hold their fire for fear of wasting ammunition. Opposite (below) a river which wanders through Virginia, flows near Petersburg to the James and thence to the sea; a river which owns a name memorable to history, the Appomattox.

Grant's forces opposing Lee in the lines at Petersburg, numbering more than double the Confederates, felt secure in their entrenchments. Time, and every other factor that favors a larger, much better supplied army, was on Grant's side. He could afford to probe and parry, push his lines gently this way and that, yet withholding the overwhelming attack that was always expected. The Union soldiers, well fed and well clothed, seemingly had time for things like this game of cards, broken up by a bomb tossed into the middle of the levity, and pictured here in lithograph. This Northern piece, entitled "The Interrupted Game," was meant to portray the still-villainous intent of Confederates. Though Confederate soldiers also played cards, this served to advertise to many the overwhelming strength of the Federal army, an army which had time for "cards and refreshments" without denuding the picket lines or embarrassing the commissary.

Among Grant's soldiers there was quiet confidence. They thought they now had positive knowledge of what before had been merely one more rumor of war. Tales were spread about Union scouting parties surprising small groups of Confederate soldiers who would fire one or two rounds and then try to get away. Prisoners taken revealed this: No more ammunition. Surely the "Rebs" couldn't hold out much longer, and brigades boasted to one another as to who would be first marching into Richmond's Capitol Square.

The Crater, depicted in this pen-and-ink drawing by Sheppard, had
been caused by the explosion of a gigantic land mine—which had taken
nearly five weeks to excavate—at the Petersburg lines. The blast dug a
great hole in the ground, 175 feet long and more than 60 feet wide and
to a depth of nearly 35 feet in some places. The hoped-for effect was to
so startle the defenders that simultaneously attacking Federal forces would
be able to breach the imposing land-trenches and fortifications with which
they were faced. The explosion did surprise the Confederates, and some
of their men were killed. But when Union troops rushed forward into the

Crater, they found themselves in a death trap, pinned down by fire from all sides. And when reinforcements were sent to exploit what the Union commanders surely thought was a breach in the Confederate lines, they joined the mass of men already milling in the devastated no man's land of the Crater, amongst the dead and dying, broken artillery pieces and rubble. The Northern scheme was a failure, and after casualties and captives had been totted up, the situation before Petersburg was much as before.

Military wisdom might have dictated abandonment of the capital, but General Lee, in conference with President Davis, had been advised that Richmond, symbol of the Confederacy, could not be given up. There was nothing for Lee to do but go back to his freezing trenches and hold the Petersburg line as long as he could.

Finally, inevitably, Lee had to fall back at shelled and gutted Petersburg. Amidst the terrible ruin of war the same brave soldiers who might
have said: "We'll fight the Yankees till hell freezes over and then we'll
fight 'em on the ice," now seemed to guess what lesser destiny fate had in
store for their cause.

This wounded Zouave, in his once gay uniform of baggy scarlet trousers, white gaiters and embroidered jacket topped off with a sort of fez, sits forlornly in a nearly deserted camp waiting for medical attention like many others on both sides. Those still fighting, particularly the ragged soldiers in Confederate ranks facing the Union lines, needed help too. The increasing use of repeating rifles gave an enemy, already overwhelmingly superior in manpower, an even greater edge in firepower. And Union sharpshooters had weapons with telescopic sights which brought uncanny accuracy to long-range shooting. Grant was growing stronger by the day as vast supplies from City Point flowed in an unquenchable stream to his troops in the field.

In addition, well-stocked medical supply boats like the one below, tied up at Appomattox Landing, made ministering to the Union wounded and sick easier. Lee determined to attack Fort Stedman, knowing that if the onslaught were successful, he would be able to cut the railroad to City Point and thereby sever the chief supply route.

The attempt, though courageously pushed, failed for the usual reasons. Reinforcements did not arrive when or where they were supposed to because of transportation breakdowns; the Northern troops regrouped in force faster than had been expected, and at least one Confederate detail suddenly found some of their guns would not fire because of defective ammunition.

-·◦·⊰{ CHAPTER TEN }⊱·◦·-

ROBERT E. LEE carried two banners toward fame and immortality. First, as a soldier, he was a leader of supreme ability, highly successful by any measure of that profession. Second, he was a man of great mental capacity, of rare integrity and spiritual force. There are those historians who believe Lee suspected from the beginning that the cause of the South was virtually hopeless. He was certainly a man who by intellectual gift had to see a fact for what it was without disguising reality behind the wishful thought. Yet once he had carefully examined his conscience and chosen his course, resigned his command in the United States Army and donned the gray, he wholeheartedly dedicated all his great military wisdom and intuition to further the Confederate cause. General Lee emerged from the War Between the States not as a vanquished commander, but as one of the great heroes of American history, and the admiration felt for him throughout the North was no less sincere than the affection he inspired among all people in the South. Other men fell from favor on both sides. The two Presidents, Davis and Lincoln, were vilified in their own camp, as well as the enemy's. Other commanders, North and South alike, knew the bite of severe, persistent criticism. Even Grant and Sherman, finally to translate the overwhelming numerical and material superiority of the North into victory, were not immune. But Lee rode serenely along, respected even by those who opposed the cause he served.

Pickett's forces falling back in the face of Sheridan's onslaught at Five Forks. This followed the last desperate gamble at Fort Stedman after Pickett, with Bushrod Johnson, had attacked "the seas of Union manpower" with their little force, pushing them back to Dinwiddie Court House. But only temporarily, for Sheridan ordered a counter-

attack which swept resolutely forward to recapture lost territory, engulf a large portion of Pickett's men. Grant immediately started at the Petersburg entrenchments, and in this engagement A. P. Hill was killed. The next day Petersburg fell and the evacuation of Richmond was speeded.

$1000 | Six per cent | Nº 27878

NON TAXABLE CERTIFICATE.

By Authority of the 14th Section of an Act of Congress approved 17th February 1864

It is hereby certified that there is due from

THE CONFEDERATE STATES OF AMERICA

and payable TWO YEARS AFTER THE RATIFICATION OF A TREATY OF PEACE WITH THE UNITED STATES

unto _____ or assigns

ONE THOUSAND DOLLARS,

with Interest at the rate of Six per Cent per Annum from the _____ day of _____ 186_ inclusive payable on the first days of January and July in each year at the Treasury in Richmond, or at the Depository in _____ Mobile Ala.

This Certificate is transferable only by special endorsement executed in the mode endorsed hereon, and the Principal and Interest are exempt from taxation

ENTERED _____   Richmond, Marc 9 1865

RECORDED P.Z.G   _____
                                   REGISTER OF THE TREASURY.

Leading up to the last desperate months of the Army of Northern Virginia, there had been equally foreboding happenings on the home fronts. The Congress of the Confederate States, meeting in what was to be its last session, debated such ticklish problems as whether to arm the slaves and send them into battle. "With two hundred thousand Negro soldiers in the Union Army, can we hesitate longer?" asked Governor Smith of Virginia. Economic problems were also perplexing. Rumor had it that Memminger did not know exactly how much had been circulated in the way of government notes. Bonds, made non-taxable as a public lure, were issued to siphon off the treasury notes, some of which were repudiated, causing further distrust in the economy. A dollar in gold would bring one hundred Confederate dollars. In the North, McClellan, deposed army commander, had made a run as Democratic candidate for President, as that party claimed that the war was a failure. Meantime a cartoonist in *Southern Punch* pictured Lincoln trying to mend the old Union with glue. Memminger himself was not to last in office to the end but chose resignation as the best way to balance the books.

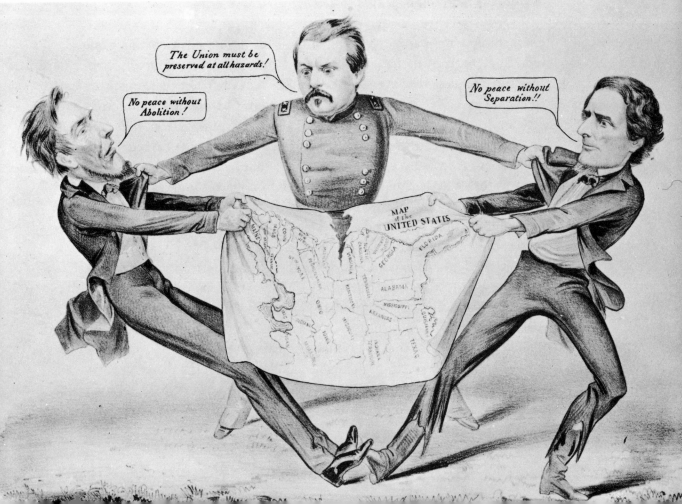

For the men excitedly debating issues in Richmond, this would be their last chance to argue at the capital. Even as they talked, the threat to their city grew. For a time the enemy was contained in the earthworks of Petersburg. The cold months of the winter slowed all activity—except the inexorable build-up of Grant's supply system and the fruits thereof. But the repulse at Fort Stedman and the defeat at Five Forks on April 1st proved that Richmond, after so many alarms, after so many heroic defenses, could no longer be held.

On April 3rd, 1865, Mayor Joseph Mayo of Richmond sent word to the Union army at Richmond's gates: "The Army of the Confederate Government having abandoned the City of Richmond, I respectfully request that you will take possession of it with an organized force, to preserve order and protect women and children and property. . . ."

There was confusion and some panic in the city. United States troops were reportedly closing in on Richmond from two sides. No citizen was sure whether they would come as conquerors and despoilers, or merely as a victorious occupying force. One wounded scout told all who would listen of the "endless lines of Union soldiers" he had seen some days before, coming forward steadily through cold rain, some of them chanting, "Richmond! Richmond! Richmond!" People with kin in the Deep South recalled stories of Sherman's march to Savannah and on up through the Carolinas, and shuddered. Soon Richmond was ablaze, fired not by the Yankees but by her own people. And into the blazing, exploding inferno came the first Union troops under General Weitzel, and soon the Confederate flag was hauled down and replaced by the Star Spangled Banner. It would be nearly five years before even Virginia's blue flag was allowed to fly again.

These two Brady photos show the ruins of Richmond. The government had long since departed, taking "the cars" from Danville station for points further South. Of the terrible fire, only smouldering ruins and tottering walls remained. Inhabitants were pleasantly surprised at the conduct of Federal soldiers; one Southern lady spoke of the invaders as "respectful." People now told one another that the war was over and that fighting had probably stopped everywhere.

But there were still Confederate soldiers and Confederate camps. Until the end of the month in which Richmond fell, April of 1865, General Johnston's men held out. Then they too capitulated to the inevitable, this time in the uniform of Sherman. Mobile, whose Confederate soldiers and encampments are shown, also surrendered. Remaining were Forrest's and Taylor's forces elsewhere in Alabama, and Kirby Smith's on the west side of the Mississippi.

On April 9th the Army of Northern Virginia fought its last battle. It was a valiant attack aimed at Union breastworks above Appomattox Court House, and everything that could be done to make it succeed was done by Lee, the other Lee, Fitzhugh, as well as by Gordon and Long-street. Some ground was taken, some Union cannon captured. But then the great might of the Federal army bestirred itself, and the thin lines of gray were hurled back. Finally there was no other course but to ask for a truce. The fact that there was no flag of truce to be found anywhere in Gordon's forces held up proceedings momentarily while a suitable substitute had to be made. The historic meeting of Lee and Grant took place in the farmhouse of a Virginian named McLean. Grant in victory

was a gracious commander, and Lee made no secret of his appreciation. Men of the cavalry and artillery who owned their horses were allowed to retain the animals, and the Northern general immediately ordered that the provisions of the capitulated army be replenished. Officers were not called upon to deliver up their side arms. Observers of that epic interview report that before surrender details were decided, the two great commanders reminisced pleasantly about old army days and other memories shared by both. When Lee finally mounted his horse outside the farmhouse, Grant courteously saluted him by raising his hat, as did all the other Union officers near. General Lee responded respectfully and rode off.

Nothing remained for Lee to do but break the news of surrender to his beloved army. As he rode among their tattered ranks, they crowded around him. This man they had seen calm in the face of defeat, humble in the face of victory. Now they watched him struggle for words. Finally he said: "Men, we have fought through the war together. I have done my best for you. My heart is too full to say more." An illustrated version of his official leave-taking of the army appears above. Meantime the Confederate Government, shorn of its brightest shield, was still attempting to carry on. Acts of government were signed by the roadside (opposite) and there was some talk of "joining Johnston." But the end was in sight for civil as well as military authority. The last order of the Confederate Government during the first week of May appears above, while beside it a Montgomery paper hails the "Great News" that the war is at an end.

Jefferson Davis was still determined to carry on the fight, and with the remnants of his officialdom, less sure of their course now than he, went first to Danville, virtually on the border between Virginia and North Carolina. With Lee's force no longer an army-in-being, the government decided to go even further South and again officials crowded anxiously around a depot, this time at Danville. The President and the government stopped at Greensboro. Here Davis said: "I think we can whip the enemy yet, if our people will turn out."

By now the party had left the railroad and taken to the roads. At Washington, Georgia, the last cabinet meeting was held and the decision made not to continue the struggle; the Confederate States of America were no more. Finally, after farewells (left), Benjamin was to go this way, Mallory that, and only Reagan was left. Placards were being posted everywhere offering $100,000 for the capture of Jefferson Davis. Not many miles from Florida, Davis rejoined his wife. Here he was finally taken by Federal troops, and his hope of joining Kirby Smith's men, who, he felt might be willing to carry on the fight, went for naught.

To Kirby Smith's trans-Mississippi army, word had come of Davis'
capture. There was no longer a leader, a country or a cause for which to
fight. The valiant veterans of Texas and the Deep South dispersed.

The last shot of the war was fired by the Confederate raider *Shenandoah*, which had continued to cruise the seas only to find out about the end of the war weeks after the fact from captured newspapers.

With the last shot fired, the actual fury was ended. But the shadow of war was not easily dispelled. Bitterness born of defeat and hunger went with the tired men of the disbanded Southern armies as they trudged back to once-familiar lanes and fields, those small dear places now ravaged perhaps, or beaten into strangeness by the destructive hand of conflict.

The terms imposed on the Confederates were fair in many respects. Sherman, like Grant, had been generous in victory. But Lincoln's assassination worried many thoughtful Southerners. Most of them would have preferred him to the fire-breathing men who now acted in his stead, some demanding "full punishment of the Rebels."

Lincoln, many believed, was preparing a peace of reconciliation, and his attitude toward the Confederate states was characterized by a degree of generosity and liberalism certainly not shared by all in his government. Some of the Confederate leaders were summarily incarcerated. Jefferson Davis, himself, was imprisoned and held in solitary confinement at Fortress Monroe, his suffering earning him every day more sympathizers in both North and South than he had ever boasted as President.

To a South in need of rehabilitation, its means of caring for itself—manufacture, transportation, and financial system—all in ruins, the Washington government, shorn of Lincoln's magnanimity, contributed antagonisms, wranglings and impositions founded on revenge.

But in time the South would substantially rehabilitate itself; its Confederate leaders were pardoned, though spirited Bob Toombs refused to seek such amnesty, remarking to United States officials: "I have not pardoned *you* yet."

To most people of the South the end of the war came as a relief. Even in those who still believed devoutly in the cause for which they had struggled, the urgency of war was now dulled by exhaustion. Many still remembered the comfortable, easygoing decades preceding Sumter and yearned for a return to those secure times.

For the soldiers the decision was the simplest. They had fought and fought hard. Now the nation for which they had been fighting was gone, their leaders gone. It was time to go home. To find somewhere across the tired, scarred face of the South that small piece of land they had once called home and those loved ones there who made it so. No unsettled issue of war could be as important as that.

And so they went as plain men now, no longer soldiers, to reclaim life and the land as best they could, "after four years of arduous service marked by unsurpassed courage. . . ."

INDEX

·✦{ INDEX }✦·